MIAMI BY NIGHT

Frommer's

MIAMI
by Night

BY

ERIC NEWILL
AND LAURA KELLY

WITH JOHNNY DIAZ
AND JORDAN SIMON

A BALLIETT & FITZGERALD BOOK

MACMILLAN • USA

a disclaimer

Prices fluctuate in the course of time, and travel information changes under the impact of the varied and volatile factors that influence the travel industry. Neither the author nor the publisher can be held responsible for the experiences of readers while traveling. Readers are invited to write to the publisher with ideas, comments, and suggestions for future editions.

about the authors

Eric Newill is managing editor of Ocean Drive. His writing has appeared in the *Village Voice, Premiere, Interview,* German *Vogue,* Spanish *Vogue,* and *South Florida.*
Laura Kelly currently teaches journalism at Florida International University in Miami.
Johnny Diaz, born and raised by the sun, sand, and surf of Miami Beach, has written for the *Miami Herald* and *Boston Globe.*
Jordan Simon is the author of several guidebooks, as well as co-author of the *Celestial Seasonings Cookbook: Cooking With Tea.*

Balliett & Fitzgerald, Inc.
Executive editor: Tom Dyja
Managing editor: Duncan Bock
Associate editor: Howard Slatkin
Assistant editor: Maria Fernandez
Editorial assistants: Ruth Ro, Bindu Poulose, Donna Spillane, Catie O'Brien

Macmillan Travel art director: Michele Laseau

All maps © Simon & Schuster, Inc.

MACMILLAN TRAVEL
A Simon & Schuster Macmillan Company
1633 Broadway
New York, NY 10019

ISBN 0-02-861138-1
Library of Congress information available from Library of Congress.

special sales

Bulk purchases (10+ copies) of Frommer's and selected Macmillan travel guides are available to corporations, organizations, institutions, and charities at special discounts, and can be customized to suit individual needs. For more information write to Special Sales, Macmillan General Reference, 1633 Broadway, New York, NY 10019.

Manufactured in the United States of America

contents

ORIENTATION MAP   10

WHAT'S HOT, WHAT'S NOT   12

THE CLUB SCENE   18
Getting Past the Velvet Rope (21)
MAPS   23
THE LOWDOWN   27
    Classic dance clubs (27)
    Intimate clubs (29)
    Low-key clubs (29)
    Where the boys are (30)
    What a drag (31)
    Disco fever (31)
    To take it off (32)
    Dress in black (33)
    Clubs in the 'burbs (33)
    Comedy clubs (34)

Rock 'n' roll (34)
All that jazz (36)
For folk and blues (36)
Latin nights (36)
THE INDEX   **39**
An A-to-Z list of night spots, with vital statistics

THE BAR SCENE   **48**
Liquor Laws (50)
Sources (51)
MAPS   **52**
THE LOWDOWN   **56**
Putting on the Ritz (56)
Slumming (56)
Where to take a client (57)
Brilliant boites (57)
The South Beach bar crawl (58)
Terraces with a view (59)
Other realms (60)
Mainland bars (60)
Classics (61)
Neighborhood dives (62)
Sports bars (62)
Gay bars (63)
Like, what's your major? (64)
Adult pursuits (65)
Up with coffee (65)
THE INDEX   **67**
An A-to-Z list of bars, with vital statistics

THE ARTS   **76**
Sources (78)
Getting Tickets (79)
THE LOWDOWN   **80**
The play's the thing (80)
There are no small theaters (81)
Classical sounds (82)
Congregational sounds (83)
Men in tights (83)
Promoters and impresarios (84)
Stars and planets (84)
The silver screen (85)

Latin floor shows (86)
Concert venues (87)
THE INDEX   **88**
An A-to-Z list of culture spots, with vital statistics

SPORTS   **92**
  Getting Tickets (95)
  THE LOWDOWN   **96**
    WHERE TO WATCH (96)
    Pigskin (96)
    Peanuts and Cracker Jack (97)
    Slapshots (97)
    Hoop dreams (97)
    Smaller balls (98)
    Playing the puppies (98)
    WHERE TO PLAY (98)
    Biking (98)
    Ice capades (99)
    Jai alai (99)
    On the run (100)
    Pickup places (100)
    Rack 'em up (101)
    Blading (101)
    Bowling (102)
    Swimming (102)
    Batting cages (103)
    Up to par (103)
    For gym rats (104)

HANGING OUT   **106**
  Getting Your Bearings (108)
  THE LOWDOWN   **110**
    Aerial views (110)
    To see the sunset (110)
    Walk this way (111)
    People watching (112)
    Adult toys (113)
    Stargazing (113)
    For caffiends (114)
    Nosh 'round the clock (114)
    Let there be music (115)
    Drive time (115)

For cruising of another sort (117)
Fab fests (117)
The write stuff (118)
Tattoo you (119)
Flowers (119)
When the art bug bites (119)
Street musicians (121)
Storytelling (121)
Nighttime shopping (121)

LATE NIGHT DINING   126

How To Dress (129)
When To Eat (129)
MAPS   130
THE LOWDOWN   135

See-and-be-scenes (135)
Institutions (136)
For after-midnight munchies (137)
Decor to die for (138)
Local color (138)
Consistently the best (139)
Where you'll be the only tourist (139)
First class with a dress code (140)
Nouvelle done well (141)
Oceanside dining (141)
Bayside dining (142)
Best-looking crowds (143)
People watching (144)
Isn't it romantic? (145)
Where Elvis would have eaten (146)
Cheap Italian eats (146)
Cuban food (147)
Caribbean food (148)
Sushi (148)
Asian delights (148)
You say you've been dying for some alligator? (149)
Cheap eats from south of the border (149)
Where the portions are larger than Montana (150)
For sports fans (150)
Best-looking crowds in docksiders (151)

THE INDEX   152
An A-to-Z list of restaurants, with vital statistics

Airports (165)

Airport transportation (165)

All-night pharmacies (165)

Babysitters (165)

Car rentals (165)

Credit cards (166)

Crime tips (166)

Doctors (166)

Driving around (167)

Emergencies (167)

Festivals and special events (167)

Gay and lesbian resources (169)

Miscellaneous resources (169)

Movie hotline (169)

Newspapers and magazines (169)

Opening and closing times (170)

Parking (170)

Public transportation (170)

Radio (171)

Smoking (171)

Taxes (171)

Taxis (171)

Tickets (172)

Time and temperature (172)

Tipping (172)

Trains (172)

Traveler's aid (172)

TV stations (172)

Visitor information (172)

Miami Area Orientation

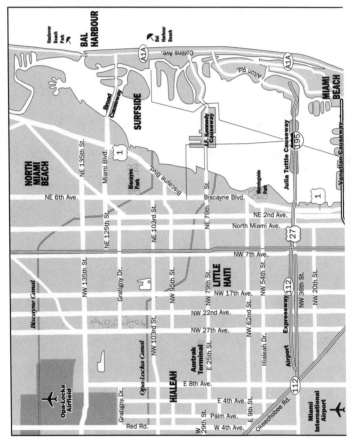

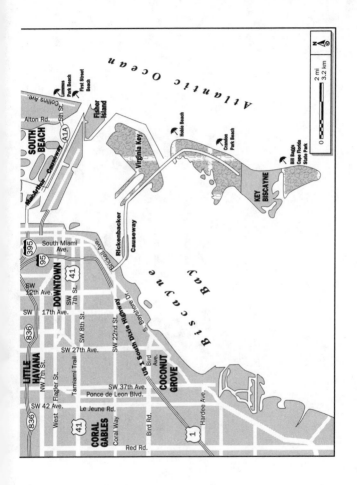

what's
hot,
what's
not

Once upon a time there existed a steamy swamp swarming with alligators and mosquitoes, home mainly to Seminole and Tequesta Indians. Then, three charismatic—and mercenary—visionaries appeared on the scene. First came Julia Tuttle, a glib, attractive widow who had inherited 600 acres of this prime land in 1891. Next was Henry Flagler, a railroad baron seduced by Mrs. Tuttle's schemes and dreams of a new playground for the rich, famous, and bored. Finally, came George Merrick—a 1920s cross between Walt Disney, Billy Graham, Philip Johnson, and the Sultan of Morocco—who designed the USA's first planned community, the fancifully fancy Coral Gables.

These three entrepreneurs built Miami into the delicious den of (mostly innocent) iniquity it remains to this day—and night. Gangsters, showgirls, snake-oil salesmen, and just plain snowbirds dripping with dough flocked to this fantasy creation. That fun in the sun and spark in the dark continued through the 1950s, the days when Jackie Gleason, Aly Khan, Frank Sinatra and his Rat Pack, and Bugsy Siegel made it a regular stomping ground. But then as the world grew smaller, the jet set took off in search of newer, more exotic locales. The Miamian profile grew older; it seemed to lose some of its sheen, becoming the butt of Catskill comics and the focus of DEA officials.

Then, in the mid-eighties, the one-two punch of the Armani-jacketed "Miami Vice" juggernaut in conjunction with the dusting off and revitalization of art-deco South Beach, restored the sparkle and sizzle. It seemed that overnight a neglected neighborhood of grit and grime had become as glam as a *Vogue* photo shoot. The arbiters of style and their slavish followers of fashion pronounced Miami reborn. And today a parade of night-creeping creatures slithers from one hot spot to the next, enjoying the wild multicultural stew, from Cubano exiles in guayaberas (those loose cotton shirts so necessary—and stylish—in the sultry air) to drag queens in gowns. And so Miami is once again a steamy place swarming with predators and prey—but now most visitors don't seem to mind getting bitten as the night devours them.

What's hot

Flesh and fame... In the midst of the sensational South Beach renaissance, Miami is again riding high—in some ways, higher than ever. The late eighties arrival of the fashion-modeling and entertainment industries have brought to the town a stunning array of gorgeous people; arguably no other city on earth has more pure beauties per capita. (If this sounds shallow, well, it is. But remember: no one is entirely immune to the lure of physical perfection; when you're wallowing in it, you'll see what we mean.) In the wake of these glamour industries has sprung a wealth of restaurants, bars, and nightclubs with a truly world-class tone. After all, if such local royalty as Madonna, Calvin Klein, Cher, and Sylvester Stallone are going out here, they *must* be entertained in the manner to which they're accustomed.

Ultra hot spots... First-time visitors are shocked when they see how urbane this place is. Media hype aside, they still expect a cross between God's Waiting Room and Belmont Park, not a glimpse of Kate Moss and Johnny Depp in the recesses of the chic-est club south of Battery Park. As these things go—and they sometimes go very quickly—the hottest spot in town is Ian Schrager's Delano Hotel, a blindingly white mating and meeting ground for the terminally famous. Lobby cocktails or dinners on the verandah are de rigueur. As for nightclubs, Madonna pals Ingrid Casares and Chris Paciello reign over the most highly touted spot to hit town in years—**Liquid**. Meanwhile, old standards, such as **Bar None** and **Groove Jet**, are still hyperbolically "in" (see The Club Scene).

The melting pot... A true melting-pot city that has achieved character through the genius of its mix, Miami is also an unofficial capital of Latin America, and so presents one of the world's hottest Cuban and Latin scenes. Additionally, South Beach has become a major destination for gay travelers because of the equally red-hot clubs, bars, and special events catering to that crowd. (See The Club and Bar Scenes.)

Chemical Cubanisma... Though the culture of cigars and coffee seems to have hit throughout the world, it never left Miami in the first place. Power Cubans and hip international swingers have always done better with a few jolts of caffeine and nicotine, and everyone else here seems to have figured it out. Not only do these two "ups" fuel lasting nocturnal forays, but—more importantly—they embody the luxury and aristocracy of old Havana that has become a nostalgic subtext for so much of Miami. Of course, leather banquettes and cognac help set the tone (see the Bar Scene). But, no matter the setting, the wise visitor forgets about being politically correct and strikes a match to his or her evening with a stogie (they come in many different sizes) and a cafecito.

Easy access... Miami Beach is a walking town, with a rigid urban grid system to its streets, thus making it a joy simply to wander around until you see something you like. Without the messy bother of cars and squalid shopping plazas, *New York* magazine's "SoHo in the Sun" appellation is perfectly suited. Visitors of any stripe are handily sated here; locals are delighted that one of the world's great scenes can be found mere steps from their door. (See Hanging Out.)

Drag queens... If *The Birdcage* weren't proof enough (although that film hardly captured the engaging if squalid reality of the thing), South Beach is one of the country's foremost capitals of drag. Not only do drag queens populate gay nights at clubs, they seem to be everywhere else as well, from straight hangouts to restaurants to benefits to supermarket openings. These regional RuPauls even turn up in the ads for major Florida departments stores. And it's no wonder—the South Beach drag queens are innovative and hilarious; they have created a psycho world full of creative characters—from Adora to Kitty Meow—that are a long way from the old lip-synching-to-Judy-Garland school.

Lincoln Road... Though much-photographed Ocean Drive continues to lure out-of-towners with its frenetic beat—and certainly deserves the glare—at certain peak times it can seem that all that's left is tourists staring at other tourists. Those who want to escape these moments and see the real South Beachites at play should go to legendary Lincoln Road. Founded as the actual epicenter of the Beach, in its glory the Road was the "Fifth Avenue of the South," complete with Saks, Bonwit's, furriers, and swank movie palaces. Today, it has regained a mood of chic, as style setters and the generally pulchritudinous parade up and down, popping into a cafe for a bite or settling down at one of the streetside bars for a long winter's binge. No cars are allowed on the "mall," which, with the plethora of galleries and boutiques, boites and theaters, makes it a pedestrian's paradise.

What's not

Scarface imitators... Though Miami was indeed a festering drug capital in the seventies and eighties, and though illicit substances are still found here as they are everywhere else, the romantic notion of Al Pacino stuffing his nose in a mountain of white powder has faded from the nightlife—and culture—scene. So if you're in any way hoping to become a Colombian Cocaine Cowboy while in wide-open Miami, you should rethink your plans. After all, it's not only illegal, but terrifically passé in terms of club culture.

Surf 'n' turf... Indigenous cuisine—beautiful seafood bathed in infused sauces mixed with tropical and Caribbean fruits and vegetables—has come to Miami, so unless you're with grandma, please avoid the 5pm steak-and-lobster-dinner-for-$12.99 joints. The town's tastes have grown up, and new-wave Floribbean cuisine has put South Florida on the culinary map. It may still be hard to find a progressive piece of theater here, but we certainly have better food than Chicago does. (See Late Night Dining.)

Attentive service... It's not the kind of thing the Chamber of Commerce likes to own up to, but it's true. Generally, restaurant service is awful in Miami, especially in South Beach. Think of it as relaxed. Changes in latitude, changes in attitude—that sort of thing. Scientists are still trying to determine the actual causes of such a widespread display of bad service, but to no avail. And to add insult to injury, many restaurants have begun to adopt the European policy of automatically tacking on a 15 percent charge to your bill.

New York attitude... Though all-powerful New Yorkers are among those credited with giving South Beach much of its renascent glamour, more and more locals have grown tired of Big Apple bitchery and carping.

True, we don't have the best service in the country, it's still hard to find Dunhills at midnight, cabbies are more surly here than at Grand Central—we know that (see above). But many of the new South Beach residents are reformed New Yorkers, and the best-behaved New Yorkers—epitomized, believe it or not, by the likes of Calvin and Kelly Klein, and Barry Diller—actually behave supremely well here, taking it all with a grain of salt and a healthy dose of sun and salt water. Miami Beach, remember, is about *not* being in New York— while still having access to its sophistication.

Coconut Grove weekends... Once a sixties bastion of hippie counterculture, the charming, rustic village of Coconut Grove has unfortunately metamorphosed over the years into a gigantic, open-air mall—which means it becomes a key teenage hangout on weekends. This is not to say that the Grove isn't a must-stop, or that everything there is below par: It still features some of the town's best restaurants and hotels, and, off the beaten track, it can still be spectacularly beautiful with its junglelike ambiance. But, on weekends especially, it is overrun with too may tykes on four wheels who are just out to cruise the streets and pick up whatever they can find. The Beach, too, is beginning to see this invasion, and though you can still have a good weekend time in either spot, you'll find these neighborhoods have much more adult panache on school nights.

the clu

b scene

1

It's 5am at the venerably
trendy News Cafe. Dazed
club kids in combat
fatigues sip mochaccinos
and wolf down feta omelets
on the waterfront patio.
Bikini-clad models so thin

it hurts Rollerblade past, backlit by moonlight. A drag queen—still in stilettos, with mascara running—walks her Great Dane. And a pair of "altakakes" (Yiddish meaning loosely "the old ones") who've made Miami Beach their home for decades promenade arm-in-arm, brandishing their canes, perhaps on the way to breakfast. Welcome to the hiphopper-than-thou South Beach (SoBe to some), proof that Miami after dark is a Twilight Zone where the X Generation meets ex-generations, and the club and street scenes are virtually interchangeable.

Indeed, "Dancin' in the Streets" might well be Miami's theme song: witness that Latino Fred and Ginger tangoing up Little Havana's Calle Ocho. There are times you wonder, why even bother paying the cover? But if you want America's coolest people watching, steamiest dancing, and hottest musical mix, venture past those velvet ropes. (Sorry, Gay Paree, Big Apple, Baghdad by the Bay, and Big Easy.) As far as the vampires who live for the nightlife—and never seem to have, or need, day jobs—are concerned, Miami is IT, the top, precisely because it's so over-the-top, its parade of characters verging on parody. (Perhaps that explains the dearth of comedy clubs in Miami—this city *is* a punch line.) And the supreme irony of it all is that what started as a beach resort for mature snowbirds now features a nightlife whose sheer flamboyance and youthful exuberance are as much a sightseeing attraction as anything under the South Florida sun.

SoBe is the flashy arriviste on the nightlife see-and-be-scene: club kids with shaved heads and multiple body piercings rubbing elbows (and God knows what else) with the likes of Madonna, Marky Mark, and Sly Stallone. It also helped sparked the renaissance of rock clubs, where bands play a musical grab bag from grunge to garage, reggae to rave. But Miami's vaunted reputation as the hot spot for the next wave of music and musicians is exaggerated. If anything, the city's self-proclaimed status as the next Motown or Seattle lies in its Latin roots. Locals Gloria Estefan and Jon Secada have actively encouraged young Latino talent; some of the best venues to hear their recycled, remixed salsa and merengue are, predictably, in Little Havana.

This Cuban enclave (and the nearby dowager communities of Coconut Grove and Coral Gables) could just as well be another world away from SoBe, across the causeways and on what club kids sneeringly call "the mainland" (not that they don't love "slumming" in the Latino clubs). In fact, despite the constant flow of poseurs and mere wannabes back and forth, you can step back into a virtual time warp in Miami proper. The old-fashioned clubs in Little Havana resemble a colorized version of Ricky Ricardo's Club Tropicana, where aging Latino couples relive the glory years of pre-Castro Cuba, politely ignoring the gyrations of Americanized kids with their slicked-back hair, muscle Ts and spandex dresses the color of tropical frozen drinks. Few experiences match hearing such greats as Celia Cruz and Tito Puente, or rising Latin jazz flutist Nestor Torres, amidst a truly appreciative audience unafraid to stomp their feet in more ways than one.

The elegant supper clubs in the Grove strive desperately to duplicate the days of the El Morocco and Stork Club, putting on the ritz. The scene is usually a sea of stuffed shirts, black ties, and overly beaded gowns of the sort that only look good in a black-and-white 1930s comedy. It's more gaudy and garish than glam, but no less fun to watch (until the check arrives). The Grove and Gables even host a few defiant little jazz, blues, and folk clubs—and hotel lounges—where nicotine and alcohol, not herbal Ecstasy, remain the drugs of choice.

Of course, no industry is as volatile as the club world, and these various haunts come and go like travelers in an airport. As such, some of the following establishments may no longer be plying their nocturnal trade by the time you peruse this volume, so it's important to call first or check local listings. On the other hand, many are institutions and continue season after season to set the energetic pace that others follow. And you can always count on a new crop of blazing newcomers, building upon the Beach's past successes and creating fresh trends and traditions. You can always check the free weekly, *New Times*, for listings; even the chicest clubs keep it on the rack. After all, there's nothing wrong with free publicity, and as they say in the Miami club world, "We're all whores, honey. Only *some* of us get more free drinks."

Getting Past the Velvet Rope

South Beach is much like New York in terms of dress and attitude (including door attitude). Although the weather is hotter, and less clothing is certainly an option, professional clubgoers still rely heavily on black and wouldn't be caught dead in shorts, the wrong T-shirt, or any similarly provincial garb. After all, it's still a sophisticated urban center with a renowned international flavor, and people dress here as they do in any other hot spot. Photographers, you see, are everywhere.

22

This philosophy is important to remember when trying to crack the velvet rope. Look confident, secure, and appropriate, and you'll eventually have no trouble. Beauty, of course, helps, so if you're not picture-perfect at least try to go with someone who is. If that, too, is hard to find, then put together your most up-to-the-minute—while still subtle—ensemble: Darker clothes blend in best (although the occasional neon hue also works, especially for women). Basically, try to do anything possible to enhance your sex appeal, from short dresses to form-fitting jeans for guys. Remember that this is a town run on good looks. If you're arriving from some distant spot where night looks haven't quite entered the 1990s, at least watch MTV and see what the various VJs—if not performers—are wearing.

Though doorman bribes are not unknown when entering clubs, it's a policy that must be handled deftly. Not everyone takes bribes, and those who do are not willing to take them obviously. The best option is to forgo such a tactic unless you are an old hand at it elsewhere. Similarly, doormen hate name-droppers ("I'm working on Madonna's new video"); it doesn't matter if what you say is true or false because so many people in town are doing things that in one way or another relate to the glamour industries that your acquaintance with designer X or star Y means nothing unless you're with them. Unless otherwise noted, cover charges vary. Call ahead to find out the price.

MIAMI ☾ THE CLUB SCENE

Coral Gables, Coconut Grove & Little Havana Clubs

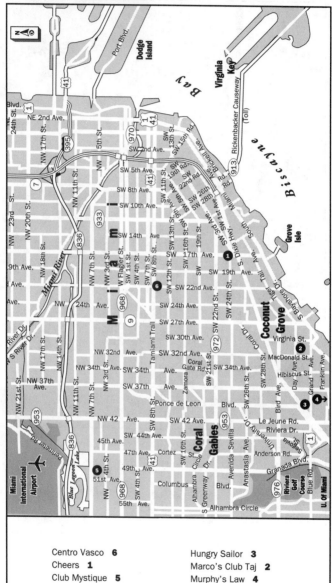

Centro Vasco **6**	Hungry Sailor **3**
Cheers **1**	Marco's Club Taj **2**
Club Mystique **5**	Murphy's Law **4**

Miami Area Clubs

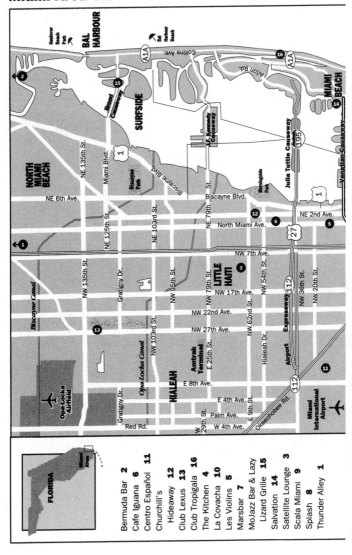

Bermuda Bar **2**
Cafe Iguana **6**
Centro Español **11**
Churchill's
Hideaway **12**
Club Lexus **13**
Club Tropigala **16**
The Kitchen **4**
La Covacha **10**
Les Violins **5**
Marsbar **7**
MoJazz Bar & Lazy
Lizard Grille **15**
Salvation **14**
Satellite Lounge **3**
Scala Miami **9**
Splash **8**
Thunder Alley **1**

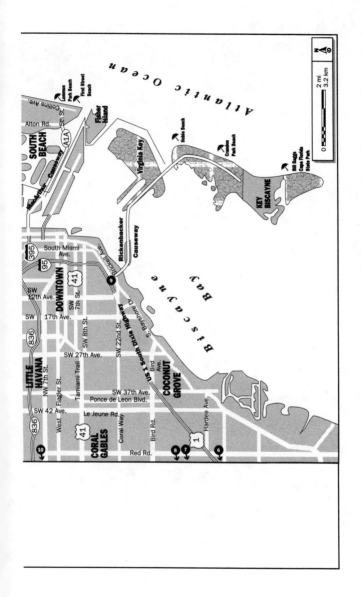

South Beach Clubs

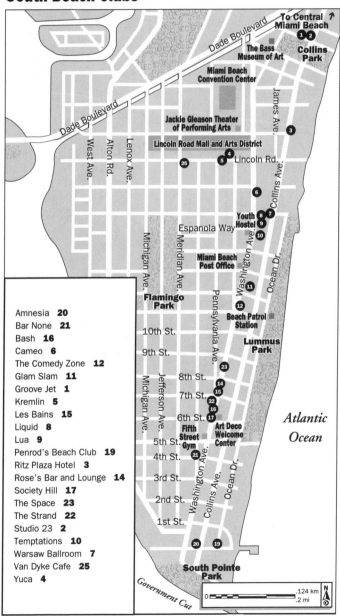

Amnesia **20**
Bar None **21**
Bash **16**
Cameo **6**
The Comedy Zone **12**
Glam Slam **11**
Groove Jet **1**
Kremlin **5**
Les Bains **15**
Liquid **8**
Lua **9**
Penrod's Beach Club **19**
Ritz Plaza Hotel **3**
Rose's Bar and Lounge **14**
Society Hill **17**
The Space **23**
The Strand **22**
Studio 23 **2**
Temptations **10**
Warsaw Ballroom **7**
Van Dyke Cafe **25**
Yuca **4**

The Lowdown

Classic dance clubs... When people talk about South
Beach nightlife, they are usually referring to the
immense pleasure palaces of dance, those soaring, throbbing caverns where the beautiful people meet one
another and, by the end of an evening, may be wearing
more attitude than clothing. Most of these clubs play
up-to-the-minute music by the likes of Madonna, and
so walk the line between trendy and cutting edge.
Among the numerous, quickly changeable haunts-of-
the-minute is **Liquid**, the relatively new celebdome
owned by Madonna pal Ingrid Casares and club vet
Chris Paciello. In addition to the regular record-release
and model parties held here, every night offers a caval-
cade of the town's most highly placed and highly
defined stunners. Dark and dreamy, the club is located
above the street at one of the Beach's busiest intersec-
tions, allowing stalled traffic a long gaze at the immense
lines of would-be revelers waiting to get inside. Once in,
it resembles most other clubs (at least the ones with
purple banquettes), but it's the scene that matters. The
VIP room is perhaps the town's most difficult to enter,
which makes it all that more enticing, even if nobody's
there. On the other hand, that could be k. d. lang chat-
ting up David Geffen, couldn't it? This mix of publicity,
beauty, style, and celebratory abandon is what made
South Beach, so any club hoppers worth their drink
tickets wouldn't dare miss this one. **The Strand**, one of
the initiators of the South Beach renaissance, still pulls
in a stunning variety of hip locals, models, European
photographers, Hollywood actors, and Manhattan
socialites. Circular booths, lots of arches, mirrors, and
backlighting give it a look of no-nonsense élan, and the
menu's classic, too—American and Continental stan-

dards served up with a nouvelle flair. Another bastion of fun is **Groove Jet**, the wildly popular club operated by Beach club giants Greg and Nicole Brier, whose more intimate Velvet made their name a few seasons back. (Velvet, now closed for renovation, is scheduled for a rebirth soon, so check current listings.) Groove Jet is everything a nineties club should be, simmering with the best music, secluded nooks, a more sedate secondary room, and a wide-open terrace that allows guests to soak in the balmy, starry, Miami sky above. Though located a bit north of the city's main streets, the club has only used this fact to its advantage, setting itself apart from the melee and practically taking over the neighborhood with a bevy of energetic kids. Meanwhile, the venerable **Les Bains** continues to rake in the crowds. An offshoot of the famous Parisian club Les Bains Douches, the establishment is located in a landmark Washington Avenue structure that is highlighted by an enormous early-sixties free-form construction, which, apparently, once advertised the merits of a long-departed bank. Proceeding from this Jetsonian device inside, club goers are blanketed by the walls of television sets and speakers seemingly erupting from the walls. The crowd tends to fall more into the Euro/Ibiza set that took up residence a few years back, but nights vary, so, again, it's wise to see what's on the menu before ordering. Finally, speaking of the Euros, **Amnesia** overcame its unpopular pioneer status in a basically residential neighborhood, and is now thriving, surrounded by such other off-the-beaten-track hangouts such as La Voile Rouge and Penrod's. With a sister club in Saint-Tropez, Amnesia is an open-air funhouse situated on a number of levels, all of which are decorated with a forest of potted plants and odd, rather suburban sofas and furnishings. When it opened, one sly wag-about-town described the overall effect as the "senate floor from *The Planet of the Apes*." Nevertheless, the space is now a classic, and, when one is looking down from the balcony onto the pulsating dance floor, the music is right, and the drinks are heady, there seems to be no other place to be. Of course, there are better clubs in town, but this is the only one that takes full advantage of the blissful subtropical environment.

Intimate clubs... Some night spots mix the tone, allowing guests to see and be seen in comfortable surroundings, as well as languish at various bars, *and* dance. Chief among these is **Bar None**, a private club–like venue that remains a favorite of visiting film stars, directors, models, and fashion visionaries. A former hotel and then restaurant, Bar None is graced with an imposing entrance hall, featuring, among other things, the generic artwork of owner and Miami resident Sylvester Stallone. The place then flows easily into a main bar area and dance floor. A duet of VIP rooms rounds out the chic-clique feel of the place (hiding spots for intimate conversation are many). A high aerie looks out over the masses below, and a subterranean bunker truly keeps the undesirables at bay. No wonder stars prefer its cloistered privacy. A few blocks up the street and further into the nocturnal crush is **Bash**, one of whose owners is actor Sean Penn. Bash has by now weathered many a season here, which must say something for its cozy air and professionally posey clientele, although when last we looked it had maintained its air of a crumbling 19th-century Italian train station, which was all very chic in the early 1990s but is becoming less so. Nevertheless, good-looking people still abound, drinks still flow, and no one seems the wiser. Up on charming Española Way, a tiny side street off Washington that was fashioned in the 1920s to resemble an exotic Caribbean city, sits **Lua**, stuffed with overstuffed chairs and hung with well-hung mirrors. So cozy that when the tiny place is full, patrons must step around and over their peers to practice the art of air-kissing, Lua is a perfect venue for champagne and romance. The air of a Victorian parlor à la Nell's completes the mood.

Low-key clubs... Of course, in a resort town noted for its nightlife, there are always a few less high-profile spots that still keep the disco lights burning until dawn. **Penrod's Beach Club** is a well-known name in these parts, being one of the first clubs to open in the newly hopping Deco District, but by now, in a new location at the tip of Ocean Drive, it's rather long in the tooth and frequented by guzzling frat boys (of the variety who fancy themselves future CEOs). Still, an outdoor area provides refreshing Atlantic views and breezes. On the up side, a new club called **The Space** has the younger crowd of causeway-crossing kids jumping about until the wee hours with its well-honed mix of high-energy music, multilevel hangouts, and key Washington Avenue location. This is a great, no-nonsense spot for classic fun—without the hype and pretentiousness that mar more publicized venues.

Where the boys are... South Beach has become one of the world's gay capitals, and as such offers a scene that compares with any on the globe. Indeed, the gay clubs are so good that many progressive straight people accompany their friends to indulge in the general hedonism. Perhaps the best space in town, **Glam Slam** (now owned by The Artist Formerly Known as Prince), is a throbbing palace carved out of an old movie theater. With an immense dance floor, a gargantuan lobby, and a swirling deco staircase leading to an oversized balcony, the futuristic architecture provides the perfect backdrop to the sweaty scene. World-class DJs and light shows allow patrons to become completely engulfed in the moment. The club will soon be in the hands of the legendary **Warsaw Ballroom**, the granddaddy of Miami gay clubs and one known internationally throughout the circuit. Located a few blocks away in a deco gem, Warsaw has for years been the site of bacchanalian revels that last until dawn. In addition, performers from Grace Jones to RuPaul to Boy George have made it their South Florida stomping ground when they are in town. Meanwhile, the recently opened **Salvation**, housed in a former fish market on the Beach's west side, is rapidly becoming one of the community's favorite places to play. The industrial milieu and rather forlorn location combine to give it the air of a dark and mysterious hideaway, exactly the type of mood necessary for full-scale abandon. Again, the music is top-flight, a mix of dance and trance that will bring on the occasional moment of emotional and sensory transcendence. On Lincoln Road is the rather humorously decorated **Kremlin**. Although an imperial palace from the time of the czars may never have served as the theme for a gay disco before, it seems to work here. At the very least, dancers don't seem to notice, obsessed as they are with each other and the beefy Argentine and Brazilian go-go performers who seem exotically out of place against the odd White Russian decor. Away from the Beach, the gay set pack **Splash**, but, unlike its more spectacular cousins, this anonymous little slice of a place could be in any town throughout the contiguous 48.

What a drag... Your friends can drag you in against your will or, if you're feeling bold, you can just get those lime-green sequined pumps and that old blond wig out of your closet and make a grand solo entrance of your own. If you opt for the sequins on a Sunday night, you'll feel right at home at **Amnesia**, an open-air disco in South Beach. This is where the grand divas congregate to trade makeup tips and writhe regally on the dance floor; even grander divas, the likes of Damien Deevine, Wanda, and Daisy Dead Petals, also throw some wild shows. Don't stand too close to the stage when they perform, though—they've been known to hurl chicken legs or squirt juices on their adoring fans. On Monday nights, many of the same powdered faces that grace Amnesia pop up again at **Caffè Torino**, a dimly lit South Beach restaurant with a stage that a dozen queens call home. The audience sits and eats dinner while the "girls" do their thing on stage. Wanda, a towering black queen with a snow white hair wig, tends to make grand entrances and exits. One time, she arrived at the restaurant perched on top of a taxi. If you want to have fun on the mainland, catch a taxi (make sure Wanda's not on top) to **Splash**. It's not wet but it can be wild, largely because of Betty Butch, who hosts the Monday night drag show. But beware. Whatever you do, *don't* interrupt her! If you do, honey, Betty'll read you like a book.

Disco fever... For the best alternative scene (in addition to **Groove Jet**'s splendid Sunday event, The Church, the weekly rave scene of the progressive, all-in-black set) check out the **Kitchen**, an industrial dance and Gothic club that sets the innovative Design District aflame every Friday and Saturday. An extraordinary crowd, fashioned in exquisite ensembles, creates a neo-Victorian/futuristic mood that provides its own edgy high. Funeral wear is fine, capes are encouraged, and arriving by horse and buggy shows the proper spirit. Meanwhile, the drug-fueled seventies and eighties saw the nightclubbing height of junglelike Coconut Grove, and though the drugs are more or less gone and the Grove is no longer Miami's Nightlife Central, **Marco's Club Taj** is endeavoring to recapture those lost evenings of Studio 54 glamour. An ornate entrance, complete with a nearly nude female statue, greets visitors, assuring them that this will be a sumptuous, if mildly vulgar, step back to true high living. Unlike the Beach, here patrons dress to the nines, knowing that their version of discoing entails jewels, high heels, short dresses, and jackets for the gents. A variety of levels competes with the guests for sheer ostentation, champagne buckets adorn most tables, and the blinking, twinkling lights flash on and off like airport runway signals. No matter—this is Miami at its best and worst, and a helluva fun time if you're in the mood. Though the more sedate town of Coral Gables is not necessarily known for kicking up its heels, the Hyatt there does host **Alcazaba**, a typical spot for the pursuits of top-40 and salsa. Nobody could call it innovative, but it's the only game around if you're stuck in the Gables sans auto and are desperate for a late-night twirl.

To take it off... Beautiful women bare it all in nothing but stiletto heels and a bow in their hair at **Club Madonna** on South Beach. This faux-posh palace, bedecked in blue and pink glowing lights, attracts wide-eyed 18-year-olds as well as slightly more senior (though not necessarily less wide-eyed) gentlemen out on the prowl. A dozen women perform each night, employing a variety of techniques: They jump and gyrate on couches, twirl around poles, or sit on your lap. Outside a white limo with the club's logo sits parked, waiting to roll. When the club opened two years ago, material girl Madonna threatened to file a lawsuit, contesting the use of her name in the club. Women aren't the only ones who take their clothes off in Miami. At **La Bare** in North Miami Beach, professional dancers named Sebastian, Manny, Louis, Eddie, Rene, and Giovanni, to name just a few, work their female audience into a screaming frenzy on a nightly basis, and collect a lot of dollars in their jock straps while they're at it. Name your fantasy, ladies: Cowboy, fireman, policeman, or hunky farm hand, La Bare has the finest specimens ready to take it all off (well, *almost* all) for you. The club has been featured on that bastion

of virtuous living, the *Sally Jessy Raphael Show*. For gay
men and the straight but curious, the **Warsaw Ballroom**
on South Beach, the granddaddy of gay clubs, hosts a
weekly amateur strip contest. Gay boys and some of their
slightly more mature brethren aspire to their 15 minutes
of fame as they expose their toned arms, pecs, legs, and
butts. Once in a while, a drunk amateur exposes something else. The crowd cheers and jeers as appropriate and
then votes for the top stripper of the night. The cash
prize is usually $100. And the losers run up their bar tabs
for the night to help themselves recover from their first
and last dance.

Dress in black... If you want to get out of the house, go to
the **Kitchen.** A gathering spot for South Florida's Gothic
club kids, here they can rebel without cause in all-black
attire. That's definitely the color—or noncolor—of choice
in the Kitchen, whether patrons are wearing T-shirts and
jeans, long coats, or dresses. If you lose sight of your com-
panions, good luck trying to find them again—the club's
interior is as dark as the revelers' clothes. Kitchen DJs
churn out the latest in industrial, New Wave, retro, and
progressive music, spinning soothing melodies by groups
like Nine Inch Nails and Ministry. The dance floor in the
back of the club is, appropriately enough, called the Dark
Room, but the strobe lights back there might actually help
you locate that missing friend (or, if you're lucky, discover
a new one). The unofficial dress code at **Marsbar** is much
the same as at the Kitchen. A haven for college-educated
Xers, alternative revelers, and nipple chicks jamming to
new wave and progressive dance, Marsbar entertains with
retro music, an ambient music room, and strange insects
dangling from the ceilings. Smack in the middle of a mall
called Town & Country, the club is nevertheless more
down and funky than most collegiate hangouts. Some
kids wear glowing rings and necklaces, probably so they
can find each other while groping their way through this
temple of darkness.

Clubs in the 'burbs... Sometimes you find yourself in the
suburbs—you're visiting friends or you're going to that
hidden-away Vietnamese restaurant. On such occasions,
Miami does provide a healthy dose of nightlife that may
make it unnecessary to cross the causeway and risk traffic

MIAMI ☾ THE CLUB SCENE

and pesky police roadblocks. In much-maligned Kendall, we find the very fun **Marsbar**, which is about as alternative as a strip-mall town is going to get. The crowd is of the wear-all-black variety, which means they would rather be in some bohemian slum than the ironically named Town & Country shopping center, but the bar hops to a groovy beat once you're inside. Edgy songs from new wave to today's MTV "Buzz Bin" emanate from the speakers, allowing a semiotic dose of true otherness to overtake the room. Highly recommended if you're in the area. More predictable is **Cafe Iguana**, which, surprisingly enough, is located in the very same Town & Country center (rather like one-stop nightlife shopping for the urbanly challenged). Nights and moods here range from retro to Latin to Garth Brooks, so come prepared for a melange. In any event, the scene can be fun with enough liquid bracers, and the watery deck out back is a nice respite from the crowd. Up north, meanwhile, is the **Bermuda Bar**, which is nothing if not energetic. Wild Women's Wednesday sets the tone for the weekend, which usually involves a load of guys looking for the pickup of their dreams and a bevy of ladies seeking true romance and a chilled Malibu rum shot. It is advisable to dress down here, as you may otherwise be mistaken for an auto valet.

Comedy clubs... Once fertile ground for comedians from Jackie Gleason to Jerry Lewis, Miami has lapsed into a sour middle age. No, not really—everyone's too busy dancing. Still, there is certainly a dearth of comedy clubs in town. At press time, there is only one: **The Comedy Zone**. But it *is* pretty hot. Top talent from around the country regularly stop by this Washington Avenue laugh lounge, and the patrons exit with smiles you'd never see in dance clubs. In addition to name stars from television and Las Vegas, The Comedy Zone laudably offers many starting comedians (some local) readying their acts for the big time. Add to this a great (and *very* busy) bar and a comfortable atmosphere, and you won't really mind when the frat boy next to you laughs till he nearly pukes.

Rock 'n' roll... Miami has a bustling local music scene, and that, combined with the regular appearance of name stars, has contributed to an explosion in the number of live rock clubs. Chief among these is the **Cameo**, the Washington Avenue deco showplace that over the years has hosted everyone from Marky Mark to that secular Amy Grant, Sophie B. Hawkins. Also one of the Beach's most frenetic and largest dance clubs, the Cameo is basically the haunt of the young and restless. Beautiful kids who could easily populate the next CK One ad (Calvin would love it) stream in to launch their own, updated Lost Generation. Meanwhile, **Rose's Bar and Lounge** is a smaller, more publike venue for pop, rock, and alternative groups in a lodgey setting that could easily serve as an after-hours joint for the Royal Canadian Mounted Police. Last on the Beach is **Society Hill**, which mixes its live acts, some of which are quite good, including the ever-popular Solomon Grundy, with a DJ in a series of lost-youth-gone-yuppie-attorney nights. Again, the look is Bar Standard. Off the Beach, **Cheers** has gained the loyalty of the University of Miami crowd with a jambalaya of local bands, Latin rhythms, and reggae that seems to perfectly capture the subtropical allure. To the north, **Thunder Alley** serves the young Aventura crowd in North Miami, a batch of groovy if somewhat suburban people dancing to a hip DJ, and occasional live acts that really get the place hopping. A true Miami great, however, is **Churchill's Hideaway**, one of those all-things-for-some-people spaces that offers not only a nice lineup of local and national rock acts (all on their way up), but also a mix of folk and poetry, not to mention Wednesday's multimedia filmscreening night. Though the Hideaway part of the name is appropriate (it's located off Biscayne Boulevard, in a rangy neighborhood), so much the better for the club's fans, who like the mood of clandestine romance. In Coconut Grove is the venerable **Hungry Sailor**, which lives up to its former-hippie-enclave setting by providing a laid-back, seductive mix of rock, reggae, and alternative by more-than-competent bands. The crowd is a cross-section of college students, young professionals, and die-hard rock addicts, all of whom roam the subtly nautical space with sexy ease. Finally, as a nod to Miami's rural roots, we have **A.J. Roxx**, which sponsors such events as Grateful Dead tributes. If you're into that kind of stuff, go with someone bigger and stronger.

MIAMI ☽ THE CLUB SCENE

All that jazz... Not a typically jazzy town, Miami never-theless has acquired over the years some pretty decent haunts in which to experience the silkier side of musical heaven. Chief among these is the **MoJazz Bar & Lazy Lizard Grill**, which nightly features the best horns and bass south of New Orleans. Indeed, this is truly the afi-cionado's hangout, where the entire point of the evening is the music. Tucked away on a less frenzied stretch of Miami Beach, MoJazz is renowned for luring the nation's best for a set or two. Though the neighborhood can be a bit dicey, it's worth a cab ride to travel to the **Satellite Lounge**, an Overtown landmark for more than 30 years. Velvet paintings and famous conch fritters set the stage for legendary blues artists like B. B. King. Check local listings to see who will be stopping by. The **Van Dyke Cafe** on Lincoln Road is not chiefly thought of as a jazz club—it's really the street's key meeting place for a nosh and a chat. But if you make it upstairs to the plush sec-ond level, you'll find patrons reclining on Victorian sofas while a number of solid-to-good singers and artists per-form. As this goes on every night, and as one can't be upstairs and miss the acts, it's a wonder more people don't go just to hear the star players. A cunning bar at the side allows for discreet conversation.

For folk and blues... For something different—espe-cially in Miami—fans of the blarney love **Murphy's Law**, an Irish pub in Coconut Grove that nightly pre-sents a liberal smattering of folk music from the Emerald Isle, as well as a hearty selection of traditional dishes. No mango conch fritters here! Meanwhile, R&B enthusiasts head to **Club Lexus**—in an out-of-the-way neighborhood where shootings are not unheard of—a real *joint* that provides some of the town's most soulful (and soul-searching) sounds.

Latin nights... Now here's something Miami excels in. No other city in the country explodes as powerfully with the rhythms, sounds, and dances of Latin America as this one. Of course, the beat is primarily Cuban, resounding electrically with the mood of old Havana. From full-scale floor shows reminiscent of Batista-era hotel shows to small clubs reverberating to a more modern mix, Cuban performances thrive. In addition, for not only the professional nightclubber but also the amateur sociologist, these clubs represent a culture that is at best difficult to encounter anywhere else. No visitor to Miami should allow a trip to pass without encountering one of these hot spots. Our mini-tour should start with the evergreen **Centro Vasco**, a brilliant establishment located in the heart of Little Havana's Calle Ocho. Here, splendid performers evoke the Lost Island to the roaring approval of the emigre patrons, many of whom were among the original refugees from Castro's Communist revolution 35 years ago. Though the decor borders on kitsch, it shouldn't be taken lightly, as it represents years of angst and memories for those involved. Nevertheless, Centro Vasco is a supremely happy place: The sublime Cuban delicacies and splendid shows are reason enough to celebrate. One of the club's former attractions, the vibrant Albita Rodriguez, has made quite a name for herself since escaping from Cuba with her entire band three years ago. Since then, she has become a major presence on the roster of Gloria and Emilio Estefan's record label, which also includes Jon Secada. Now, she is practicing her version of crossover (she still performs exclusively in Spanish) with Thursday and Sunday appearances at **Yuca**, the nouvelle-Cuban Valhalla on Lincoln Road. Not only does Yuca present some of the most intriguing variations on classic island cuisine, it also offers one of the town's most haute scenes as well. Power types are seated everywhere, enjoying cigars, food, and the sounds of Albita. On a smaller scale, the **Ritz Plaza Hotel** on Collins Avenue offers evenings of Cuban and Latin rhythms where visitors can soak up the sultry subtropical ambience. Speaking of hotels, the legendary Fontainebleau may not be renowned for its Cuban-ness, but it now presents a grand floor show on the order of high-glamour 1950s Havana. The **Club Tropigala** is today's version of Ricky Ricardo's Tropicana, the venerable nightclub from "I Love Lucy." Showgirls, bedecked in feather headdresses and little else, regale a champagne-woozy crowd with the lusty lures of old Cuba (or old Miami Beach). Somehow, we think Sinatra would approve. Similarly splashy, but with a great deal more verisimilitude, is the famous **Les Violins**, which has reigned on Biscayne Boulevard almost since Fidel first came down from the hills. Owned by a venerable Cuban family, it is everything you could imagine: elegant patrons, more bejeweled chorines, heavy supper-club fare, stiff cocktails, the works. Absolutely a must-stop on anyone's tour of vintage Havana transferred to southern Florida. Meanwhile, **Scala Miami** also offers a slightly more scaled-down but nonetheless amusing show infused with Caribbean touches. On the other hand, Miami also hosts a slew of Latin discos, where the salsa and merengue spin all night. One of the most popular, despite its odd airport location, is **Club Mystique**, where hoards of beauties flock to dance away the urban blues. On the Beach, a more upscale (even stuffy, if that can be said of a Latin club) alternative is **Temptations**. Perhaps no truer mix of Miami Beach exists: The club is housed in an old synagogue that for five seconds was the darling of the yuppie playground set until it transformed itself into a very ultra and costly Latin lounge. Still, power players abound, the mood is seductive, and the club's look is striking—two levels of plush and sensory sensation. On the other end of the spectrum is the downright rural **La Covacha**, located in far West Dade. Here is a true Cuban favorite, set on a plot of land that, during quiet moments, allows one to hear the nearby cows mooing in the distance. However, there are few quiet moments: Incredibly casual kids from Little Havana, Hialeah, and beyond grind about with beers and croquettas under a chickee hut (think Gilligan's Island) until those aforementioned cows come home. Colombians prefer **Studio 23** off Collins Avenue, which gathers together the young and lively set from that beautiful South American country for evenings of catch-up, heat-up, and cool-down. Finally, over personal favorite is the outrageous **Centro Español**, known locally as The Waterfront, located at a bend in the Miami River. No words can describe this scene, which could only occur in the cultural melange of Miami. Nominally a friendly, riverside dock bar and eatery, it speeds up after midnight with the oddest assortment of patrons: Gay Latin boys dance to salsa next to Cuban grandfathers with their granddaughters; steamy lesbian couples smooch next to a young couple on their first (or second, maybe) date; a family matriarch barks food orders while her progeny whirl about under a canopy of stars. The music screams, the people are brilliant and, once you've found it, you'll never want to go home. Truly the best this town has to offer in one catch-all package.

The Index

A.J. Roxx. Live music hits the spot at this down-home honky-tonk that simply screams Alabama. Grateful Deadheads provide character.... *Tel 305/891–9019. 14075 W. Dixie Hwy., North Miami.*

Alcazaba. If taking a whirl around a hotel disco is your thing, go to it. Those in the know believe Coral Gables is more for fine dining and cocktail chatter, but who knows? You may be stuck without a car. The decor: hotel disco. The people: hotel disco.... *Tel 305/441–1234. 50 Alhambra Plaza, Coral Gables.*

Amnesia. Large open-air club that gives away its Saint-Tropez roots. Self-billed as a "disco mall," this multilevel, multiroom space features restaurants and a great dance floor under the stars, not to mention loads of potted greenery like they used to have in those eighties salad-bar eateries. Still, a number of big-time entertainment companies have their launch parties here, so you never know which star you might see. Also, the legendary Foam Parties are still packing them in on Thursdays for a wet 'n' sexy time.... *Tel 305/531–5535. 136 Collins Ave., Miami Beach.*

Bar None. One of the Beach's most *in* spots, Bar None continues to attract the upper reaches of celebrity with its purely personal service. Frontman Nicola sets the tone, a comfy interior with lots of intimate nooks works well for those with romance, gossip, or business on their minds, and the double-trouble VIP room concept (one with a view of the masses from above, one below in a self-contained secret bunker) has driven at least one nightlife columnist insane wondering what is going on in the other room. A must.... *Tel 305/672–9252. 411 Washington Ave., Miami Beach.*

Bash. Though owner Sean Penn doesn't appear often, he still lures many of South Beach's most frenetic club goers on the celebrity-appeal ticket. One can't discount its longevity, however, and that says something in the club world. Immensely comfortable and plush, though the early-1990s luxe air could use freshening. Above all, it remains one of the Beach's key scenes. Super back garden.... *Tel 305/538–2274. 655 Washington Ave., Miami Beach.*

Bermuda Bar. The young professional/college crowd loves this place for its no-nonsense approach to club life. Nothing scary here, just a bunch of nice suburban kids having a nice suburban time. Wild Women's Wednesday, which features few wild women, does entice lots of guys without dates.... *Tel 305/945–0196. 3509 N.E. 163rd St., North Miami Beach.*

Cafe Iguana. This something-for-everyone club—retro, rock, Latin, even country—reigns supreme in the hinterlands. Its strip-mall location comforts the patrons, and it does lure a lively bunch come Friday and Saturday. Thankfully, the waterfront back patio offsets the creepy name.... *Tel 305/274–4948. Town & Country Center, 8505 Mills Dr., West Kendall.*

Caffè Torino. Some dozen drag queens regularly invade this South Beach restaurant to lip-synch their favorite tunes. The Monday night drag shows, which feature, among others, Wanda, Taffy, Cocoa, and Marvela, draw a lot of locals from their homes (if not their closets).... *Tel 305/531–5722. 1437 Washington Ave., Miami Beach.*

Cameo. An institution on Washington Avenue, Cameo carries on its successful mix of young, hot kids, great live national acts, and a steady bass beat. This restored old deco theater was one of the first clubs to signal the South Beach renaissance, and it's still going strong. Those under 25 love it, but you might feel a little wizened if you're approaching 28. By the way, the key to the name resides in a detail on the building's 1930s facade.... *Tel 305/532–0922. 1445 Washington Ave., Miami Beach.*

Centro Español. One of Miami's most bizarre and beautiful scenes. Located on the bank of the Miami River, Centro

Español metamorphoses itself from a daytime dock and food stand to a blazing all-night party. Though primarily Latin, all comers are welcome. Neither the hour nor your age, nationality, or sexual preference matter: Cuban families dance next to blistering gay couples until the wee hours. For sustenance, do a beer and a tamale. And bring a boat if you have one.... *Tel 305/635–5660. 3615 N.W. South River Dr., Miami.*

Centro Vasco. The days of old Cuba are recaptured here in the heart of Miami's Little Havana. If Calle Ocho is the main thoroughfare of the city's Cuban community, this club is the street's jewel. Fine island cuisine, authentic decor, and true survivors of Castro's revolution serve as the setting for amazing, electric performers. Nowhere else in the States will you find this kind of scene.... *Tel 305/643–9626. 2235 S.W. 8th St., Miami.*

Cheers. Area bands and rowdy crowds set the tone for this happy, favorite locals' bar. A number of University of Miami students mix well with old Miamians and Florida newcomers. Always a pleasant surprise.... *Tel 305/857–0041. 2490 S.W. 17th Ave., Miami.*

Churchill's Hideaway. Rock and alternative bands take the stage at this subtle boite that truly is a hideaway. Fans can't stay away from the easy atmosphere, the nice selection of beers and drinks, and the publike friendliness of everyone involved.... *Tel 305/757–1807. 5501 N.E. 2nd Ave., Miami.*

Club Lexus. Great nightspot for R&B fans. A little distant, but worth the drive if you're into the groove.... *Tel 305/687–9924. 12901 N.W. 27th Ave., Miami.*

Club Madonna. Not Madonna's club—although her lawyers apparently had an unsuccessful tussle with the place—but home to some dozen truly beautiful showgirls who bump and grind for the customers. No alcohol is served.... *Tel 305/534–2000. 1527 Washington Ave., Miami Beach. Open every day from 6pm to 6am.*

Club Mystique. Once you're inside, this hotel disco belies its white-bread location. As one of the town's best Latin DJ hot

MIAMI ⏻ THE CLUB SCENE

spots, Club Mystique draws great-looking crowds who come from throughout Miami to blaze away the night.... *Tel 305/265–3900. Miami Airport Hilton, 5101 Blue Lagoon Dr., Miami.*

Club Tropigala. The legendary Fontainebleau Hotel, once the preferred setting for Sinatra's Rat Pack, now hosts Miami Beach's most splendiferous Latin floor show. And we do mean floor show: Showgirls in feather hats a million miles high (and without the burden of much clothing) strut about like the Cuban Revolution never happened. A true trip back in time, made even more so by endless magnums of champagne.... *Tel 305/672–SHOW. Fontainebleau Hilton, 4441 Collins Ave., Miami Beach.*

The Comedy Zone. This is Miami's only comedy club. Odd, really, considering the great bouts of humor the town has inspired. Still, with a club this funny, there's really no need for another. National and talented local acts set up the punch lines like dominoes, and the *extremely* festive audiences knock them (and their drinks) down with almost alarming enthusiasm.... *Tel 305/672–4788. 1121 Washington Ave., Miami Beach.*

Glam Slam. Though currently owned by The Artist Formerly Known as Prince, this immense pleasure place is now being operated by the famous Warsaw, Miami's most lasting gay disco. The space—a former movie castle simply awash in gorgeous deco detailing—is multilevel, and includes a dramatic staircase, tremendous balcony, and perhaps the best sound and light systems in town. Spacey nights have often given way to even spacier mornings here, so be prepared. The steamy gay scene of South Beach has not earned its wild rep for nothing. Imperative: Leave your shirt at home.... *Tel 305/672–2770. 1235 Washington Ave., Miami Beach.*

Groove Jet. Royalty of the night Greg and Nicole Brier continue to host one of the town's most fab scenes. When asked where the beautiful people go, we tell them Groove Jet. Because it's everything a Miami Beach club should be—hip music, hot decor, cozy nooks, great bar—it's no wonder that models, photogs, fashion giants, and film stars make it a regular stop when they're in town. Apart from them, everyone else is merely gorgeous. Hang out on the super back terrace for a chill…. *Tel 305/532–2002. 323 23rd St., Miami Beach.*

Hungry Sailor. Live music fits the bill at this nautically themed establishment in the heart of old Coconut Grove. Rock, reggae, and blues go nicely with the mellow mood. Locals aplenty, as well as cool tourists…. *Tel 305/444–9359. 3426 Main Hwy., Coconut Grove.*

The Kitchen. Fridays and Saturdays bring out the industrial/gothic kids to this dark, dreamy warehouse space in the burgeoning Design District. The trance works, so if you're suitably vampiric, enter the temple. A great scene, and much more loving than innocents are led to believe…. *Tel 305/754–0777. 3701 N.E. 2nd Ave., Miami.*

Kremlin. Anna Karenina was never like this. Though the decor is pre-revolution czarist, the parade of Brazilian go-go boys and pumped-up patrons belies the look at this fun gay club. More manageable than most, Kremlin is perfect for just-out kids and their cute friends, not to mention the rest of the gay world. One Manhattan power broker couldn't get enough. Lots of comfy nooks, too…. *Tel 305/673–3150. 727 Lincoln Rd., Miami Beach.*

La Bare. The name says it all. Some of South Florida's hunkiest and most sculpted male strippers gyrate and grind to get the women wild and crazy. Sorry, guys, no men allowed. We tried. Only ladies over 18…. *Tel 305/945–6869. 2355 Sunny Isles Blvd., North Miami Beach.*

La Covacha. Way out west lies this secret chickee hut of a club, populated mostly by blissful Cuban/Latin youth. Though it was a place to be seen for the South Beach jet set of 1993, it has evolved into a great, relaxing hangout for kids from Little Havana, Hialeah, and surrounding districts. Another only-in-Miami winner…. *Tel 305/594–3717. 10730 N.W. 25th St., West Dade County.*

Les Bains. This heavily Euro outpost of the famous Paris nightspot is still thriving, though its *très* eighties feel can be draining. Leather-jacketed smoothies with scented Gitanes and black-miniskirted femmes fatale continue to play their scenes from *Breathless*; as the saying goes, 50,000,000

Frenchmen (and women) can't be wrong.... *Tel 305/532–8768. 753 Washington Ave., Miami Beach.*

Les Violins. This traditional Cuban club from the glory days of old Havana is a wonder in 1996. Lovingly run and splendidly decorated, its musical floor shows continue to be a mainstay on Biscayne Boulevard.... *Tel 305/371–8668. 1751 Biscayne Blvd., Miami.*

Liquid. Absolutely the hottest club in town—but, of course, that may change. What won't change is its aura of indisputable chic and glamour, largely provided by owners Ingrid Casares and Chris Paciello, not to mention their celebrated friends. Floating above Wash and Española like a permanent VIP room, Liquid has it all: beauties, great music, a super-private private lounge, and an air of impenetrability (which, of course, makes it all that more alluring).... *Tel 305/532–9154. 1439 Washington Ave., Miami Beach.*

Lua. This small boite on charming Española Way continues to get the right crowd with its overstuffed decor à la Nell's—comfortable sofas, intimate clusters of chairs, discreetly shaded lamps—which calls to mind nothing so much as a decadent parlor in some Tennessee Williams melodrama. Still, the music is on target, the people are gorgeous, and the mood is that of a private and very secret club.... *Tel 305/534–0061. 409 Española Way, Miami Beach.*

Marco's Club Taj. The random excesses of Miami's eighties live on at this large Coconut Grove pleasure emporium. The South American contingent is vast, as are those whose view of what a disco should be still resides in decades past. Nevertheless, it may be the Grove's most hopping scene, and the intrigue of lots of loose and easy money never fails to beguile. Champagne flows, dancers boogie-oogie-oogie, and everyone dresses up a lot.... *Tel 305/444–5333. 3339 Virginia St., Coconut Grove.*

Marsbar. This alternative hangout in the 'burbs belies its strip-mall location. Marsbar is actually very hip, with a smart, searingly pop-oriented clientele; if it were on the Beach it would be one of the town's hottest scenes. As it is, it's an oasis of nihilistic chic in the world of the two-car garage.... *Tel 305/271–6909. Town & Country Center, 8505 Mills Dr., West Kendall.*

MoJazz Bar & Lazy Lizard Grille. Miami's premier jazz club, MoJazz nightly brings in the top men and women in the biz. One night it's New Orleans, the next Chicago, the next maybe a little old Harlem. Obviously, the music's the thing here, and the faithful make their way to this secluded corner of upper Miami Beach with lusty eagerness.... *Tel 305/865–2636. 928 71st St., Miami Beach. Closed Mon. Cover charge.*

Murphy's Law. Irish-flavored pub in the Grove. Easy, sure, and floating on the folklike sounds of the Emerald Isle, not to mention a bit of rock and R&B thrown in for good measure. Wide beer selection; friendly crowd.... *Tel 305/446–9956. 2977 McFarlane Rd., Coconut Grove.*

Penrod's Beach Club. An old South Florida name in pleasure, Penrod's has not only planted its flag in Fort Lauderdale but was also one of the first to occupy newly happening South Beach. Ten years later, it's still kicking, with a low-profile bunch of kids who are just out to have fun, drink beer, go surfing, and parade those bronzed bodies while dancing up a storm.... *Tel 305/538–1111. 1 Ocean Dr., Miami Beach.*

Ritz Plaza Hotel. One of the less trumpeted of the larger deco hotels, the Ritz Plaza sits back calmly in the Delano's shadow and handles scores of fashion production teams and film crews. In addition to models-a-rama swarming through the lobby, the Ritz offers Live Jazz Thursdays, which, combined with the sultry deco ambience, conjures images of Joan Crawford on the make for a millionaire in pre-war Miami.... *Tel 305/534–3500. 1701 Collins Ave., Miami Beach.*

Rose's Bar and Lounge. Rose's continues to be one of Washington Avenue's key venues for live music, hosting an eclectic mix of rock, pop, alternative, R&B, and reggae. The casual atmosphere eliminates the need for dressing; T-shirts and jeans are the rule, and a lot of heavy dating action goes on between sets. Energetic and fun.... *Tel 305/532–0228. 754 Washington Ave., Miami Beach.*

Salvation. This newcomer to the Beach's gay scene is regarded by many who should know as their favorite. South Beach legend Louis Canales is the guiding hand, and his genius permeates the mix of the world's hottest men, all in varying states of undress, going through their elaborate mating ritu-

MIAMI ⏵ THE CLUB SCENE

als until the Sunday dawn. When the music begins its build, one can almost envision a blissful, trancelike end of the world. The climaxes are shattering, and patrons are completely lost in the moment. A world-class triumph.... *Tel 305/673–6508. 1775 West Ave., Miami Beach.*

Satellite Lounge. An Overtown legend, this raw blues bar would be a cliche if it weren't so great.... *Tel 305/759–9068. 6222 N.W. 7th Avenue, Miami.*

Scala Miami. This elaborate Latin floor show carries on the traditions of old Miami Beach. The rhumba, the beguine, and the mambo may have seen better days, but it's still a wacky, enlivening scene that is so rare it seems beautiful. Only in Miami (or Rio).... *Tel 305/371–5604. 905 S. Bayshore Dr., Miami.*

Society Hill. Typical South Beach scene, with typically great South Beach kids having a typically moody/sexy time in a typically dark Avenue hangout. Fun 'n' easy.... *Tel 305/534–9993. 627 Washington Ave., Miami Beach.*

The Space. New South Beach venue that seems to be getting the right mix of kids, especially on weekends. Hot DJ sounds get the place steaming. Decor is—surprise—dark. Great name.... *Tel 305/674–0408. 841 Washington Ave., Miami Beach.*

Splash. Gay dance club in the outer reaches. Nice suburban kids dancing to old Donna Summer. There's no reason to avoid it, but there's no reason to rush there, either.... *Tel 305/661–9099. 5922 S. Dixie Hwy., South Miami.*

The Strand. There at the beginning of the South Beach renaissance, this restaurant continues to draw the fashionable crowd to its venerable booths.... *Tel 305/532–2340. 671 Washington Ave., Miami Beach.*

Studio 23. The Colombian beat—salsa, merengue, cumbia—plays well into the night at this Latin hideout on upper South Beach. Dark, sexy, but it helps to be Colombian or into the scene.... *Tel 305/538–1196. 247 23rd St., Miami Beach.*

Temptations. Fancy Latin disco in the shell of an old synagogue. Brilliant space, rather fussy clientele. Head to the balcony, order a magnum, and watch the South American world go by. Live acts often perform tropical rhythms. No jeans, please, says the management.... *Tel 305/534–4288. 1532 Washington Ave., Miami Beach.*

Thunder Alley. Suburban club that hedges its bets—R&B, rock, and Latin sounds are all on the bill. Still, if you're singing the blues in North Dade County, there are worse things than an evening here.... *Tel 305/933–9003. 3025 N.E. 188th St., Aventura.*

Van Dyke Cafe. This key Lincoln Road meeting spot and eatery also features some really fine jazz upstairs on the cozy and secluded second level. Sink back into a plush armchair or sofa, order a stiff gin and tonic, and reacquaint yourself with the brothers Gershwin. Truly pleasant. Downstairs, speakers carry the musical motif from above while allowing for more conversation.... *Tel 305/534–3600. 846 Lincoln Rd., Miami Beach.*

Warsaw Ballroom. This legendary gay dance club has become known throughout the world for its quintessential South Beach mix: Great-looking men from Cuba, New York, and Europe (not to mention the rest of the globe) stream here to dance, show off their pecs, see Grace Jones, chat up Madonna, and cruise. After all these years, it may be the perfect dance club. A chic balcony—in sweeping deco— offers intimacy. Everybody welcome.... *Tel 305/531–4555. 1450 Collins Ave., Miami Beach.*

Yuca. This groundbreaking nouvelle-Cuban restaurant has brought a new power scene to Lincoln Road. In the shadow of Sony's Latin music headquarters, owner Efrain Veiga has created a Cuban cabaret, featuring the sizzling Albita on Sundays and Thursdays. Cigars, innovative takes on traditional island cuisine, electric performances, and a heavy-hitting clientele make this one of Miami's foremost haunts.... *Tel 305/532–9822. 501 Lincoln Rd., Miami Beach. Reservations necessary.*

MIAMI ⟨ THE CLUB SCENE

the bar

scene 2

Drinking has been a
Miami pastime since the
beginning, being one of
the few varieties of
entertainment available to
the pioneer set. Town
fathers also found that a

lush variety of lubrications encouraged early vacationers to spend more money than they might have otherwise.... Today, with the nightlife scene having practically outstripped fun in the sun as Miami's top draw, bar culture has mushroomed into *the* way to go on power and ego trips. It's every bit as aggressively trendy and wildly varied as its clubbing cousin.

For some revelers, the bars are merely pit stops before, between, and after clubs—a place to idle their engines. (Certain SoBe hangouts hold the eerie hush of sudden evacuation once the discos rev up.) Then there are those, of course, who merely seek the classic bar experience, sitting quietly (or not), getting tanked. For many others, it's a chance to soak up the ambiance and attitude of the clubs without the noise and cover charge.

Miami's social barflies come in an assortment of flashy colors. Tourists in loud Hawaiian shirts and polyester plaids are drawn en masse to the bustling watering holes where frozen margaritas whirl about in tanks the size of washing machines. CEOs and their trophy wives pose on plush sofas in high-toned hotel lounges, where a pianist plays Cole Porter medleys between haughty sneers at requests for "Melancholy Baby." Last year's frat boys (this year's junior execs) team up at the sports bars, especially now that the Heat, Marlins, and Panthers have joined the Dolphins on Miami's major-league roster (the action, however, would hardly qualify even as Triple-A). And of course, there are the SoBe flavors of the week, where you'll see simply *everyone*, darling, from a real-life Cruella De Ville, her black Fu Manchu fingernails creeping like a spider up her date's thigh, to a leather queen in a vest amply displaying his nipple clamps (and biker shorts showing off more than is absolutely necessary). Needless to say, your service staff is just as eclectic (and self-absorbed), from bartenders imitating Tom Cruise in *Cocktail* to waitress/models with legs for days and collagen-enhanced pouts.

As they say in classic barspeak: "Name your poison."

Liquor Laws

You have to be 21 years old to drink in Florida, and lately, in light of increased police watchfulness, bars and clubs have been especially diligent in checking IDs. Happily, bars and nighclubs in Florida are allowed to remain open until 4am, which usually means they shut down around 4:30. Of course, there are also after-hours options for those who still don't want to go home.

Sources

Check out the savvy columns of scenesters Tara Solomon (in the Weekend section of Friday's *Miami Herald*) or Tom Austin (in the free weekly *New Times*, out on Wednesdays) for the latest and most in-the-know comments on Miami nightlife. Since nightclubs here have been known to change name and ambience practically overnight, it's best to call ahead.

Coral Gables, Coconut Grove & Little Havana Bars

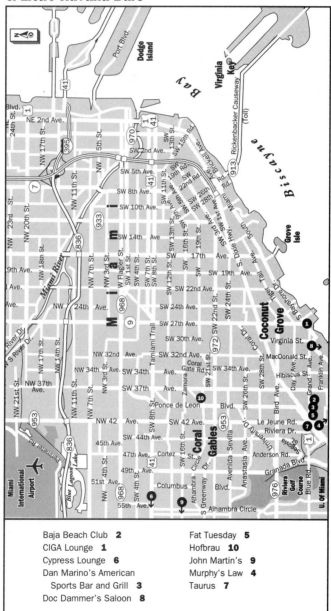

Baja Beach Club **2**		Fat Tuesday **5**	
CIGA Lounge **1**		Hofbrau **10**	
Cypress Lounge **6**		John Martin's **9**	
Dan Marino's American		Murphy's Law **4**	
Sports Bar and Grill **3**		Taurus **7**	
Doc Dammer's Saloon **8**			

South Beach Bars

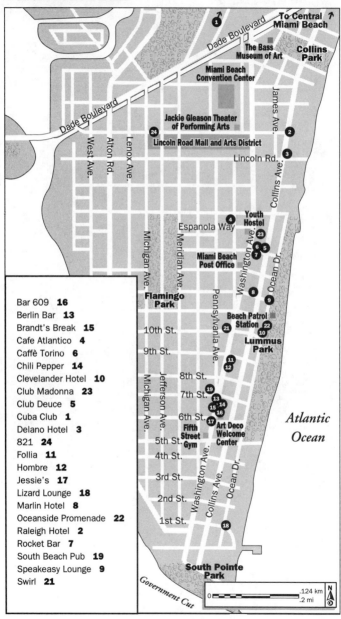

Bar 609 **16**
Berlin Bar **13**
Brandt's Break **15**
Cafe Atlantico **4**
Caffè Torino **6**
Chili Pepper **14**
Clevelander Hotel **10**
Club Madonna **23**
Club Deuce **5**
Cuba Club **1**
Delano Hotel **3**
821 **24**
Follia **11**
Hombre **12**
Jessie's **17**
Lizard Lounge **18**
Marlin Hotel **8**
Oceanside Promenade **22**
Raleigh Hotel **2**
Rocket Bar **7**
South Beach Pub **19**
Speakeasy Lounge **9**
Swirl **21**

Miami Area Bars

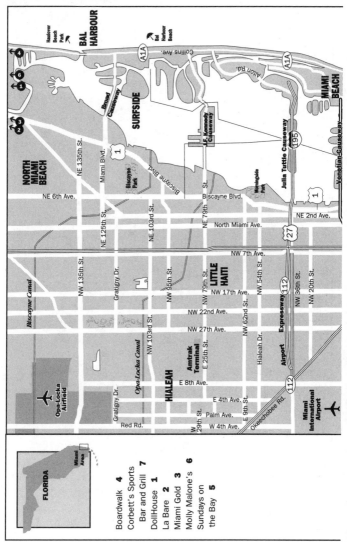

Boardwalk **4**
Corbett's Sports
Bar and Grill **7**
DollHouse **1**
La Bare **2**
Miami Gold **3**
Molly Malone's **6**
Sundays on
the Bay **5**

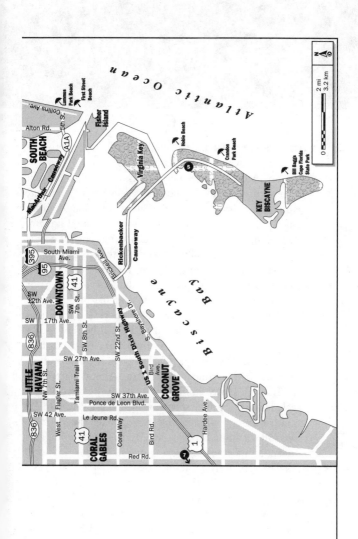

The Lowdown

Putting on the Ritz... Though Miami isn't exactly the toniest of towns, a few establishments cater to the swank set, South Beach–style. These spots draw a clientele that mixes artists, socialites, and assorted swells with models, editors, photographers, and visiting celebutantes from Manhattan and beyond. Dress? From Armani, Oldham, Anna Sui, and Versace to a fabulous vintage shift accessorized with Tiffany silver. You know the look.

Ian Schrager's South Beach über-inn, the **Delano Hotel**, is surely the chicer-than-thou establishment of the moment. Though Spanish is essential in this town, the Delano seems to hear even more German and French. One drink at the bar and you'll be ready for a party at Madonna's house. But bear in mind that Philippe Starck's decor is richer in attitude than comfort, so don't wear anything problematic. Almost next door, the **Raleigh Hotel** still presents one of the town's most secluded and hushed rooms: a tiny, spectacularly deco cocktail lounge with marble martinis on the floor. It looks like a ship's bar from an Astaire-Rogers film, and unlike in most other places, the staff does not look askance at patrons in Hermès ascots.

Slumming... If it's a dressed-down, hideout type of experience you're craving, Miami is more than willing to fill your need. On the Beach, the legendary **Club Deuce**, so famous it almost doesn't qualify, takes the title of Supreme Dive. Smack in the center of it all, staffed by charming old cocktail-keeps who really know how to mix a drink, reeking of smoke and beer, Club Deuce nightly attracts a wide mix of authenticity connoisseurs. More subtle is Coconut Grove's **Tigertail Lounge**, bathed in the shadow of the luxe Grand Bay Hotel. While during daylight hours customers can run in, down a quick rye, and get back to the office before the boss has had time to grumble, by night it becomes a true neighborhood bar, attracting those true Bukowski-ites who like plank walls and the faint smell of Naugahyde.

Where to take a client... For closing that big business deal in power-oozing splendor, nothing can rival the impressive **CIGA Lounge** in Coconut Grove's Grand Bay Hotel. Stately, impassive bartenders pour drinks straight out of *The Man in the Gray Flannel Suit*. Find a secret niche and bask in the glow of oak walls and hushed piano tones. For a more sensational display, pop by The Forge's **Cuba Club** on Miami Beach, where the old grandeur—fine cigars, leather sofas, a famous wine cellar, immense lobsters, almost obscene steaks—has lately been infused with fresh, twentysomething blood. The best of both worlds is nicely balanced here, and you will certainly find something to amuse the eye, sate the palate, and wet the throat.

Brilliant boites... Every town has to have at least one perfect bar, and in South Beach it's **821**. Barely a storefront wide, this watering hole on Lincoln Road has succeeded wildly in its short existence through an amazing mix of chic clientele, streamlined decor, the stiffest of drinks, sublime music—from lounge to retro to live cabaret—and what may be the best collection of bartenders in Miami Beach. More than anything, it's a people place, and the esprit de corps embraces all kinds: from severe Manhattan fashion editors to cute couples on a first date to gay boys in rubber shirts to middle-aged friends out for a nightcap. Every night is different, but every night is great. Meanwhile, the even newer **Berlin Bar** has everyone talking with its attempt at beau-monde respectability. Operated by two very finicky and tasteful Berliners, the room simply gleams, with its shiny black bar, looming grand piano, and flatteringly slanted mirrors. Beware: The drinks can become pricy, but the crowd is often worth it. (Fashion's Wolfgang Joop always pops by when he's in town.) Another newcomer, the **Speakeasy Lounge**, throws its eggs into that old Roaring Twenties basket and comes up with an odd mishmash, but it's one of the few secluded—not to mention seductive—places to have a drink in Ocean Drive, so it's gained a following. The fab Cotton Club look doesn't hurt, either. Meanwhile, the bar at the **Marlin Hotel** remains a favorite old standby. Rollicking along with Barbara Hulanicki's wildly colored Jamaican motif and swaying nimbly to the reggae beat, customers tend to lose themselves in one rum punch after another. Island Records entrepreneur Chris Blackwell set out in the early nineties to prove that a renovated South Beach hotel could be the chicest thing going, and the lasting success of this venture—beauties galore still tramp sexily through the lobby and order up something cold—proves why he is considered a visionary. Finally, at the tip of Ocean Drive lies the Century Hotel's wonderfully secret **Lizard Lounge**. For years the Century has been one of the Beach's most iconoclastic, brilliant venues for those in the know; the Lizard Lounge, across the street, sits directly on the ocean and caresses visitors with supreme-ly elegant casualness. Rattan chairs, glossy European fashion mags, and tall rum-and-pineapple-juices set the mood for an evening unlike any other in the States.

The South Beach bar crawl... Where, you ask, do all those pumped guys and curvy ladies go when they're not making the club scene? Answer: They inhabit the various bars along Washington Avenue, making the scene legendary with extraordinary good looks. Starting at the lower end (geographically), we find **Bar 609**, a hot spot that doesn't stop. A tiny but sexy room, it fea-tures a far-out mix of dance, salsa, and Euro techno. Almost next door—this block alone deserves a sociolo-gy book, or at least a monograph—we find the dark and mysterious **Jessie's**, which, having outgrown a long-held reputation as a hangout for Beach riffraff, has become one of the in places for slumming beauties. Beers, beers, beers are the rule, although a shot of scotch never hurt a waistline. Next, there's the immensely popular **Chili Pepper**, which is king of the hill for all the boys and girls from the nearby modeling agencies. Raucous and up, Chili Pepper practically invented the nineties South Beach mating ritual. Singles do well, and though everyone comes with his or her current amour, the night always seems to signal the end of an old romance and the beginning of an even sexier coupling. **Union Bar** started life as a British restaurant, but has, thankfully for its investors, become yet another must-call port for the genetically blessed. One block up is the obviously named **South Beach Pub**, which guarantees its existence through that old real-estate maxim, location, location, location.

(A brief word about the cluster and frequency of these bars: The scene is so intense, and the kids so eager to locate a magical night of abandon that they usually find it, and all these bars, however similar, supply the answer to this call of the wild.)

And onward: **Follia** is a restaurant—and a pretty good Italian one at that—but, like many locales on the Beach, it really heats up after the dinner plates are cleared away. Every night offers a different theme for dancing on tabletops, but professional club goers prefer Celebrity Thursdays, hosted by football great Louis Oliver, and Tuesdays, run by the extremely A-list promoter Tommy Pooch. This is South Beach the way locals like it. Finally, farther up the street, we come to a newcomer, **Rocket Bar**, a dark, dank room punctuated with spacy neon. The coolness never ends on wayward Wash Ave.

Terraces with a view... One of Ocean Drive's most-known locales—especially among tourists and inveterate causeway crossers—is the **Clevelander Hotel**, a ubiquitous sight in promotional brochures and Ocean Drive photo landscapes. Raucous, boisterous, and, at times, frankly juvenile, its seafront deck presents a great view of humanity's passing, barely clothed parade. Glass blocks and a DJ'd sound track ranging from island to rock help the place's atmosphere, but it still resembles nothing so much as a college bar transferred to an oceanfront. Nearby is **Wet Willie's**, which prides itself on atomically glowing slush drinks with curious names, such as the Call-A-Cab. Grain alcohol is the kicker here—it goes down smoothly but suddenly packs a wallop. The upper deck, also on Ocean Drive, is a prime people watching paradise. The crowd, again, can border on the collegiate, but it's a perfect pre-dinner stopping-off point if you're in the mood, with a nice view of the darkening beach and ocean. Farther up the street is the **Oceanside Promenade**, which offers a more cozy, if no less rewarding, bar-with-a-view. On charming Española Way is the more romantic **Cafe Atlantico**, where the bon vivants sip chilled whites and moody reds at cafe tables placed directly on the sidewalk. As the street is one of the town's narrowest, the willy-nilly wanderings of shoppers, bicyclists, and skaters are integral to any stop-off here. Though the interior is redolent of the Mediterranean (notwithstanding the name), the outside is better for basking in Española Way's over-the-top South American atmosphere.

Other realms... Virtual-reality games hit South Beach nightlife a few seasons ago with the popular **Virtua Cafe**. A variety of goggles-and-helmet setups can be found every few feet—some with the expected sexual escapes—in addition to a more traditional bar scene, and even a VIP room. Perhaps this signals the new wave in bar going: digitized otherworldliness cross-referenced with the ultra-unreal domain of a VIP enclave. For a virtual Emerald Isle experience, **John Martin's** of Coral Gables is the pub most likely to transport you to the other side of the Atlantic. Fish and chips and bangers and mash go quite nicely with the Irish brews on tap, and on certain evenings you might hear an authentic Irish artist strumming tunes from the motherland. If it's old Manhattan you pine for, turn instead to the Colonnade Hotel's **Doc Dammer's Saloon**, also in Coral Gables. Named for one of the town founders (no, not Clark Gable), it has the tile floors, wooden booths, jolly barkeeps, and stiff cocktails you'd hope for on a time-machine trip to Ye Olde Apple.

Mainland bars... Coconut Grove, a bastion of bohemian revelry, has a town meeting center that has been a subject of fierce debate since its construction. To some, the shopping plaza CocoWalk symbolizes everything wrong with developer improvement, trampling the indigenous, junglelike beauty of the place with a torrent of yogurt shops and obvious retailers. Others say it has given the neighborhood a viable center, providing everything one can need for a jolly day or evening on the town all in one gulp. Whatever it may or may not be, CocoWalk provides stores, restaurants, movies—and bars, which may be why it is such a hit with the young and single. Among the most popular spots is the **Baja Beach Club**, which pours on the sexual juice to an extreme. Jiggly bartendresses and cavemanlike bartenders strut their hardbodies behind the counters, doing those patented bar tricks like flipping the cocktail shakers. Televised sports games and a wet-and-wild bonhomie contribute to the overall effect of squeaky-clean degeneracy. One flight down is the Grove equivalent of Wet Willie's, **Fat Tuesday's**. Slush drinks and sloppy fun are the mainstays. Over on Key Biscayne, never known for being a club heaven, is **Sundays on the Bay**. Taking advantage of Miami's natural beauty, this home of the rumrunner and assorted other tropical concoctions is among the town's most popular weekend-afternoon hangouts, especially with those who come down to take in the sun and water. But at night, dance music keeps the mini-islanders (and visitors) dancing till the wee hours. Finally, for those who really need a bar anytime, anywhere, we have the **Cypress Lounge**. Due to its location on the Miccosukee Indian Reservation, the Cypress never closes. Though it's far west—practically in the Everglades—it does offer some extraordinary Florida color that is not to be found elsewhere. As a bar, it's rather plain; but the people and exotic location combine to make it a fun venture, or at least a refreshing spot for the eager tourist or jaded local.

Classics... The area's oldest bar, **Tobacco Road**, certainly presents the city the way it used to be. Perched downtown along the river and supported by a regular crowd of blues lovers and lager swillers, this bar is quintessential Miami. Though it has gained a degree of notoriety in the past 10 years, attracting a curious crowd of visitors who want to see what all the hype is about, Tobacco Road nevertheless maintains its unique blend of hipness and tradition. It's also a happy-hour favorite. In Coconut Grove is another venerable standby, **Taurus**. Situated on the Main Highway for as long as anyone can remember, Taurus maintains its distinction as a true old-Florida wonderland, complete with Dade pine walls, convivial bartenders, and a host of old hands clogging the bar. When the television is not blaring, visitors can glean snatches of curious dialogue about alligator wrestling and other such wacky stuff, and then, near dusk, one of the area's local bands begins to play. All in all, it's a blissful hideout, set apart in the neighborhood's leafy, jungly undergrowth. The nothing-fancy food—burgers, steaks—is great, too.

Neighborhood dives... A cut below the classics are the neighborhood haunts where loyalty is often won with good beer at good prices and dependable props like pool tables or swinging jukeboxes. The **Abbey Brewing Company** recently took over the venerable Knotty Pine, a low-key South Beach bar that had endured since 1935. The great old shuffleboard table now serves as the bar top, and the bar has started offering locals (and a few beer connoisseurs from farther-flung locales) their own microbrew products. With all the dark wood, the jazz and blues on the box, and such concoctions as oatmeal stout, this place is a great antidote to a SoBe spandex overdose. Over in North Bay Village is **Happy's Stork Lounge**, a beer joint on the eastern side of Treasure Island, just over the bridge from Miami Beach. Happy's serves up simple pleasures, especially around football time. Monday Night Football features $2 drinks during the game. Night bartenders at Happy's have been known to order in Chinese food when hungry customers get a hankering for some wings and honey chicken. Locals also rule the roost at **Big Daddy's** in Surfside. If you're sitting at the bar, chances are the bartender knows your name. Around football and ice hockey season, Big Daddy's is a good spot to catch a game, thanks to a handful of televisions and specials like 95¢ drafts. Should life lead you to pristine Coral Gables, the place to unwind with your cohort is the Germanic **Hofbrau**, a room bright with light and conversation. Sports play on the TVs, the kitchen sends out simple, satisfying fare, and next to you, you're sure to find some character with the occasional great anecdote (at least for this setting).

Sports bars... Certainly a major football star is lure enough for sports fans, so **Dan Marino's American Sports Bar and Grill** is still packing them in for a little frat-boy fun. The CocoWalk location also helps, pulling scores of shoppers and moviegoers up to the third-floor aerie for a hand at arcade games and a gander at the many televised competitions on television. Marino himself makes occasional stop-ins, thrilling patrons with his patented down-to-earth charm. Chicken wings, sandwiches, and many beers make up the standard fare. Throughout the county are other such establishments, usually more modest but equally fun. In North Miami is **Hunky's Sports Bar**, which at night dishes up live rock. To the south is **Corbett's Sports Bar & Grill**, which rounds up South Dade fans to root for the Dolphins, Panthers, Heat, or Marlins, watch innumerable other events, and dance to a classic rock sound. Even farther south, in Homestead, is the **Sports Page Pub and Restaurant**, which adds hotly battled trivia contests to the mix. The 'burbs proper features **Fat Kat's Pool Bar**, a great place to shoot some games and down a few beers before going back to the hockey final on the screen. Interactive video and trivia also make this one of Kendall's most lively nightspots, filled with people out to have a great time. On the Beach, and thus a little more surfeited with models and their glamorous accoutrements, is **Brandt's Break**, adjacent to the Chili Pepper nightclub. The pool balls fly here, shot dexterously by willowy six-footers and their brawny boyfriends. A scene, and typical South Beach.

Gay bars... South Beach has a variety of gay bars for those seeking refuge or respite from the immense clubs. **Twist** is still the town's premier meet-and-cruise bar, maintaining its title through a choice location, a staff of eager, friendly bartenders, and cool, dreamy decor. Shadowy pathways and a dark dance floor are a wonderful contrast to the easy, smooth Key West–like terrace in the back. The newer **Swirl**, where patrons span both genders and all orientations, has become a wacky alternative. Sofas, sandboxes, and toys create an open-air, under-the-stars living-room setting complete with drag queens, muscle boys, and middle-of-the-road visitors. The restaurant **Caffè Torino** also gets a widely varied crowd for its Monday Drag Nights, a South Beach tradition that's moved from place to place over the years. As the drag practiced in Miami is among the most advanced in the country, patrons are always in for a raucous, unpredictable show filled with elegant, edgy, and usually bawdy surprises. The crowd eats it up. The venerable **Hombre** still exists, but resembles nothing so much as a way station for those just off the bus. Dank and morose, it fills the sexy underbelly bill, notwithstanding a cute if tattered back garden. Finally, Lincoln Road's **West End** hosts a bevy of gay men and women playing pool and drinking another round in an airy, but somehow claustrophobic, space.

Like, what's your major?... So you insist on hanging with people who still have homework. Alright, then. The University of Miami crowd flocks to **Fat Tuesday's** in Coconut Grove, where the outdoor, second-floor, dais-like bar overlooks CocoWalk, giving the undergrads a 360-degree view of the bumper-to-bumper cruisers on Main Highway and the necklines of shoppers below. Wednesday and Thursday nights bring a tan, cruisey university crowd to **Dan Marino's** nearby sports bar. They're lured by drink specials ($3 shots, $2 domestic beers) and loud pop and alternative music. Suggested pickup line: "Heard the new Collective Soul?" College suburbanites routinely head for **Fat Kat's**, the friendly bar and pool hall in Kendall where the music lists toward AC/DC or the Stray Cats. In Coconut Grove, **Howl at the Moon** draws locals, college students, and yuppies alike who seek to celebrate the night away in off-key song.

Only in South Florida can you find an Irish pub with mint-green exteriors and pink neon signs, but on the inside (which is what counts, right?), **Murphy's Law**, also in Coconut Grove, is a cozy Dublin-style enclave with forest-green walls, a fireplace, a 120-inch TV, and some of the heartiest meat-and-potato dishes this side of the pond. Guinness, Bass, Harp, and a wide selection of other brews are available on tap. Thursday and Saturday nights lure the college hooligans, while the weekday crowd tends to be of the after-work variety. U2 imitator Thick as Thieves plays some nights; otherwise, the music is a mix of Irish folk and alternative rock. According to legend, Molly Malone sold mussels and shellfish in the streets of Dublin. Aparently she discovered the weather was better in Miami, because today she's selling Guinness, Harp, Bass, Dublin Diamond, and about a dozen other beers at **Molly Malone's** in North Miami Beach. This is the other Irish Bar in town (the glowing shamrock on the front window and the cloverleaf-green-and-white painted awning lets you know), attracting students from Florida International and Barry Universities for trivia and darts contests—or to shoot some pool. Call it a study break. On weekends, the Irish enclave draws in a mix of students, older folks, and out-of-towners. Out on the back porch, you can spot a manatee bobbing by in the Intracoastal. Fridays and Saturdays expect to hear blues singer Magda Hiller or visiting northern Florida Irish bands. The jukebox is a vault of eclectic tunes—there's even one about a girl named Molly and her wheelbarrow.

Adult pursuits... Though the nightlife of Miami and South Beach is based more on sexuality and sexiness than corresponding scenes in most other towns (perhaps due to the steamy weather, the city's hedonistic tradition, and the proliferation of beauty), there are still some spots that provide "adult" entertainment for those who want their menu plainly stated. On South Beach, there's **Club Madonna** (which has nothing to do with *her*, except that there was a scrape about the name some time back), which presents tantalizing ladies day and night. More down and dirty is **DollHouse** on upper Collins Avenue, which fits perfectly into its Motel Row setting. Wrestling matches featuring mud, oil, and cream take place in a center ring to the hooting delight of the patrons. On the mainland is **Miami Gold**, another testosterone-laden sanctuary where the women on stage do seem to really control the balance of power. The roles are reversed, meanwhile, at **La Bare**, where men take it off to the thumpa-thumpa of some old disco track while the ladies feverishly stuff dollar bills into G-strings. Heated cash-crotching also takes place at **The Boardwalk**, a noted gay establishment that's all the rage with supposedly sophisticated New Yorkers down for a tarty time.

Up with coffee... Combine the current national craze for coffee with Miami's Cuban influences and you get a city riding a caffeine high all its own. These nights, it seems there are as many coffeehouses in South Florida as palm trees. Washington Avenue's **Java Junkies** plays haven to nightcrawlers looking for something to keep them going in the wee hours. They slink in, sit down, and sip latte, or cappuccino, even mocha. They sit outside in the sidewalk cafe, munching on chocolate mousse cake, Key lime pie, fluffy apple muffins, or succulent chocolate-chip cookies. Over in the Grove, a crush of collegians packs **Joffrey's**. Brightly lit but quaint, this coffeehouse grinds out the beans even after midnight. If tables of giggly wannabes belting out their favorite Alanis Morissette hits is music to your ears, this could be your place. A few miles away, in the heart of Little Havana, bleary-eyed drivers pull over for a little taste of old Cuba at **Versailles** restaurant's coffee counter. Nothing quite captures Miami like Versailles, a genuine Cuban landmark which, for 24 years, has been at the social center of the evolving history of Little Havana: first the Cubans, then the Nicaraguans, the boat lifts, the reunions, and the rallies. Bill Clinton campaigned in the dining room; Governor Lawton Chiles worked the counters. Gloria Estefan stops by, and the popular Cuban coffee, cafecito—it can wake the dead. It's served in little paper cups, almost the size of a shot. Beware: It'll keep you up for hours.

The Index

Abbey Brewing Company. New owners recently bought out the Knotty Pine, a Miami Beach institution that had been at this location since 1935 before falling on hard times. After a face lift, this microbrew pub offers several of their own concoctions. Still low-key and mostly local, except for the occasional group of homebrew enthusiasts.... *Tel 305/538–8110. 115 16th St., Miami Beach.*

Baja Beach Club. Raucous behavior is the rule at this collegiate pleasure-fest full of well-proportioned male and female bartenders. Electric-blue shots are the standard fare, as well as chicken wings, beer, and sports on the tube.... *Tel 305/445–5499. CocoWalk, 3015 Grand Ave., Coconut Grove.*

Bar 609. Charming, dark hangout for models and locals with a variety of music from dance to salsa to Euro. Great scene, beautiful crowd.... *Tel 305/673–5609. 609 Washington Ave., Miami Beach.*

Berlin Bar. A rather over-decorated salon, but one of the town's most elegant and soigné places to be. They haven't yet gotten the music right, and the drinks are exorbitantly priced, but the mood is fine and everyone looks divine. High German mix.... *Tel 305/674–9300. 661 Washington Ave., Miami Beach.*

Big Daddy's. Like a Miami Cheers, where everyone knows your name if you are a regular. The crowds come in for "Monday Night Football" and Panther games on four gleaming TVs.... *Tel 305/866–8081. 9494 Harding Ave., Surfside.*

The Boardwalk. Brazilian boys and others strip down to barely nothing at this hole-in-the-mall for well-heeled gents. A dive, but it has a great following, even among sophisti-cates.... *Tel 305/949–4119. 17008 Collins Ave., North Miami Beach.*

Brandt's Break. Model-stuffed pool halls are quintessentially South Beach, and this is the best. Beauties bending over for that eight-ball in the corner pocket don't realize what that does for their admirers—well, maybe they do.... *Tel 305/531–9661. 619 Washington Ave., Miami Beach.*

Cafe Atlantico. Beautiful sidewalk cafe on romantic Española Way, perfection for sipping a nice chilled white while gazing at the street parade.... *Tel 305/672–1168. 49 Española Way, Miami Beach.*

Caffè Torino. Offshoot of a fine Italian restaurant in Green-wich Village, it serves as the Monday-night venue for a splendid drag revue. The show features the avant-garde of the business, so expect it to be a good deal more bawdy and innovative than an old Garland impression.... *Tel 305/531–5722. 1437 Washington Ave., Miami Beach.*

Chili Pepper. This rock 'n' roll hangout for the Wonder Crowd of South Beach is a little less fabulous than when it opened a few seasons back, but it still presents an amazing array of great kids on their way to fashion stardom, all having a good time while waiting for Calvin to call.... *Tel 305/531–9661. 621 Washington Ave., Miami Beach.*

CIGA Lounge. Named after the Italian chain that owns it, this immensely plush cocktail stop in one of Coconut Grove's swellest hotels is a perfect retreat from the mad bustle of the neighborhood. They say you can always tell how good a bar is by its nuts: Here they're huge and rich, accenting nicely the strong drinks and woodsy walls.... *Tel 305/858–9600. Grand Bay Hotel, 2669 S. Bayshore Dr., Coconut Grove.*

Clevelander Hotel. Favored spot for the hordes of tourists who pass along Ocean Drive wondering where the deco is. Caribbean/rock music calls them in to down brews on the Clevelander's seafront deck under an Atomic Age squiggle.

Sneer all you want, but it still has one of the best views of the Drive's barely dressed pedestrians.... *Tel 305/531–3485. 1020 Ocean Dr., Miami Beach.*

Club Deuce. A bar's bar, the sort of place where bartenders are ready to listen to hours of stories of heartache and loss—that is, when the curious jukebox mix of Patsy Cline and Pearl Jam doesn't interfere. Drowning one's sorrows has never been more picturesque.... *Tel 305/673–9537. 222 14th St., Miami Beach.*

Club Madonna. Tasty showgirls strut their stuff at this misleadingly named adult club on the Wash. Ave. strip. Open until 6am for true die-hards.... *Tel 305/534–2000. 1527 Washington Ave., Miami Beach.*

Corbett's Sports Bar & Grill. South Dade locals love this easygoing spot for watching the game, dancing, eating, or all three. Nothing special, but very friendly.... *Tel 305/238–0823. 12721 S. Dixie Hwy., South Dade.*

Cuba Club. Located in a venerable Beach restaurant, The Forge (home of expense-account lobsters, wines, and steaks), this bar has recently become a Thing with well-heeled South Beach playkids. Go for the cigars and scotch.... *Tel 305/534–4536. 432 41st St., Miami Beach.*

Cypress Lounge. Open all the time—and we do mean all the time—this quaint bar, located on the Miccosukee Indian Reservation, provides an exotic mix of people and locale (it's practically in the Everglades).... *Tel 305/222–4600. 5 SW 177th Ave., West Dade.*

Dan Marino's American Sports Bar and Grill. The football hero occasionally makes appearances at his eponymous sports bar, where the masses come for game watching, game playing, and jocky/comfy food and drink. Way collegiate, but fun for those who enjoy this sort of thing.... *Tel 305/567–0013. CocoWalk, 3015 Grand Ave., Coconut Grove.*

Delano Hotel. Ian Schrager's premier Miami venture is the chicest thing in town. Celebrities of all stripes mix with beauties galore. Dripping in decadent glamour, the Delano is not what you'd call comfortable, but it is extremely important. Have a drink at the 21st-century bar.... *Tel 305/672–2000. 1685 Collins Ave., Miami Beach.*

Doc Dammer's Saloon. The tiles-and-wood bar in Coral Gables' historic Colonnade Hotel presents with its stiff cocktails a little bit of Florida history.... *Tel 305/441–2600. Omni Colonnade Hotel, 180 Aragon Ave., Coral Gables.*

DollHouse. The name gives it away, doesn't it? Strippers, showgirls, and sirens give the men much more than they can handle. A landmark on upper Collins' Motel Row.... *Tel 305/948–3087. 255 Sunny Isles Blvd., North Miami Beach.*

821. Hands down, the town's best bar. A wild mix of edgy, urbane revelers makes this their nightly playground, whether the evening's sound track is a live jazz singer, retro songs from Tony Orlando, or the newest in sub-pop dance. A perfect meeting spot for any occasion, before or after dinner.... *Tel 305/532–7912. 821 Lincoln Rd., Miami Beach.*

Fat Kat's Pool Bar. Billiard tables, interactive videos, trivia games, and a general mood of conviviality make this a favorite hangout for the Kendall suburbs.... *Tel 305/274–8090. Town & Country Center, 8505 Mills Dr., Kendall.*

Fat Tuesday. Slushy drinks and a prime view of the Grove's busiest intersection lure the hoards of shoppers and moviegoers loitering around CocoWalk. Loud and boisterous. A great place to have a drink on a hot Saturday afternoon.... *Tel 305/441–2992. CocoWalk, 3015 Grand Ave., Coconut Grove.*

Follia. A classic Italian restaurant that goes gaga–South Beach with premier parties weeknights. Tuesdays bring the ubiquitous promoter Tommy Pooch's stream of models, power brokers, and jet setters, while Celebrity Thursdays are hosted by football great Louis Oliver, who likes his South Beach nightlife as well as the next guy.... *Tel 305/674–9299. 929 Washington Ave., Miami Beach.*

Happy's Stork Lounge. Nothing fancy here. Just a cigarette machine, a jukebox, bumper pool, a couple video games, and friendly, down-to-earth bartenders.... *Tel 305/868–9191. 1872 North Bay Causeway, North Day Village.*

Hofbrau. A local favorite on Coral Gables' restaurant row, this pub is the perfect spot for smoothing out a rough day or catching the game on TV.... *Tel 305/442–2730. 172 Giralda Ave., Coral Gables.*

Hombre. Once the town's hottest gay bar, darkened Hombre now lives largely off its early-nineties reputation. Still, it can provide a cool, dark spot for those humid afternoons and evenings.... *Tel 305/538–7883. 925 Washington Ave., Miami Beach.*

Howl at the Moon. Sing some songs with the piano man and a bevy of beer-drinking locals, most of whom toast and croon the whole night through (check your pitch pipe at the door). Lots of college students and yuppies.... *Tel 305/442–8300. 301 Grand Ave., Coconut Grove.*

Hunky's Sports Bar. This outpost of balls and bats is wildly popular with those living in the county's northern environs. Live rock adds diversion.... *Tel 305/653–4835. 21427 N.W. 2nd Ave., North Miami.*

Java Junkies. A pit stop for nightcrawlers in need of a recharge. Besides the regular caffeinated fare, patrons drink fruit juices and munch on rich desserts.... *Tel 305/674–7854. 1446 Washington Ave., Miami Beach.*

Jessie's. Vintage bar on Washington Avenue that's metamorphosed into a super-beauty hangout. On weekends, it's filled with causeway-crossing kids, but no matter: It's always a scene.... *Tel 305/538–6688. 615 Washington Ave., Miami Beach.*

Joffrey's. Local teens and 20-somethings pour into this Coconut Grove coffeehouse for java and tea around 11pm, and couples and first dates from nearby CocoWalk stop by at pre- and post-movie times. A local favorite: the cranberry-nut-apple muffin.... *Tel 305/448–0848. 3434 Main Hwy., Coconut Grove.*

John Martin's. This classic Irish bar has brought a bit of the blarney to South Florida.... *Tel 305/445–3777. 253 Miracle Mile, Coral Gables.*

La Bare. Ladies run amok at this Chippendale's-like strip club, where the gentlemen are the ones making a living off the currency that admirers stuff into their already over-stuffed G-strings.... *Tel 305/945–6869. 2355 NE 163rd St., North Miami Beach.*

Lizard Lounge. The Century Hotel, one of South Beach's most iconoclastic venues of chic, runs this oceanfront bar across the street. Immensely relaxing and comfortable, it features a variety of cozy rattan chairs and outdoor tables. Sublime, and a wonderful secret.... *Tel 305/674–8855. 161 Ocean Dr., Miami Beach.*

Marlin Hotel. Caribbean colors run rampant in the bar at this Island (as in Island Records) -infused hotel. Wild stools, settees, and a chic clientele add punch to the room's very nice rum drinks.... *Tel 305/673–8770. 1200 Collins Ave., Miami Beach.*

Miami Gold. Yet another bastion of the girlie show for off-duty postal workers and the like. Strippers galore with alluring names, and supposedly more alluring habits.... *Tel 305/945–6030. 50 Biscayne Blvd., North Miami Beach.*

Molly Malone's. It's one of the few places drinking college students can study manatees from the back porch. This Irish enclave draws in collegians and out-of-towners for domestic beers on tap: Guinness, Harp, Bass, and Dublin Diamond. There's a jukebox jammed with oldies-but-goodies, including one about an Irish girl named Molly Malone. Live music Fridays and Saturdays.... *Tel 305/948–3512. 166 Sunny Isled Blvd., North Miami Beach.*

Murphy's Law. Coconut Grove Irish pub with mint-green exteriors and pink neon signs, not to mention a ten-foot television screen. Home to college hooligans and a business-suited after-five set. Live rock bands perform Wednesday nights as patrons wolf down burgers and hearty meat-and-potato dishes.... *Tel 305/446–9956. 2977 McFarlane Rd., Coconut Grove.*

Oceanside Promenade. Outdoor terrace bar with a prime South Beach location. Directly across the street is the ocean—perfect for a pre- or post-drink dip.... *Tel 305/538–9029. 1052 Ocean Dr., Miami Beach.*

Raleigh Hotel. The bar in the Raleigh is one of the town's most elegant, swooning in a deco dream of high martini glasses and amber lighting. Small and intimate; the perfect date bar.... *Tel 305/534–6300. 1775 Collins Ave., Miami Beach.*

Rocket Bar. Dapper neon bar on South Beach that attracts a mass of industrial Generation Xers who'll still be partying when the sun comes up.... *Tel 305/532–7500. 1417 Washington Ave., Miami Beach.*

South Beach Pub. Another stop on the endless trail of bars up Washington Avenue. Calmer and less attitudinal than most.... *Tel 305/532–7821. 717 Washington Ave., Miami Beach.*

Speakeasy Lounge. A mad 1920s theme runs throughout this cozy hotel space, and some of the fixtures and posters are true gems. Gimmicky, but a good, secret alternative to more obvious venues.... *Tel 305/672–2579. 1230 Ocean Dr., Miami Beach.*

Sports Page Pub. The far-south town of Homestead boasts one of the area's best sports bars. Even the fairer sex gets sucked in by the game-fueled machismo.... *Tel 305/246–3633. 113 S. Homestead Blvd., Homestead.*

Sundays on the Bay. Miami's eloquent seascape makes this a fantastic day spot; at night it heats up when the DJ starts to spin, and since Key Biscayne is short on clubs, this one's good to have around.... *Tel 305/361–6777. 5420 Crandon Blvd., Key Biscayne.*

Swirl. Wild open-air antics kick this bar into the stratosphere. You never know who or what you may see, but the sandboxes, sofas, and lurid nooks are a joyful constant.... *Tel 305/534–2060. 1049 Washington Ave., Miami Beach.*

Taurus. A Miami classic, Taurus continues to please year in and year out. A Southern feel pervades the place, revealing the town's roots. Woodsy charm and talkative bartenders add warmth, and the jungly atmosphere outside makes the terrace deck additionally attractive. Husky food is served, too.... *Tel 305/448–0633. 3540 Main Hwy., Coconut Grove.*

Tigertail Lounge. Though slightly seedy, this Grove standby is a neighborhood favorite. Nothing to look at, really, but a relief from the mall-like vapidity that has overtaken the area.... *Tel 305/854–9172. 3205 SW 27th Ave., Coconut Grove.*

Tobacco Road. The city's oldest bar, this institution on the Miami River envelops you in a dark, fragrant atmosphere of blues, beer, and jocularity. Regularly voted one of Miami's best jazz bars, it attracts a mix of hip young professionals and genuine music fans.... *Tel 305/374–1198. 626 S. Miami Ave., Miami.*

Twist. South Beach's premier gay cruise bar, Twist is also a very convivial place to meet friends and while the night away. An upper outdoor deck adds a Key West feel that offsets the dark pounding of the sexy interior.... *Tel 305/53–TWIST. 1057 Washington Ave., Miami Beach.*

Union Bar. This former British restaurant has done a 180 (small wonder), landing on its feet as a great space for the beauties who populate the cosmetics ads in *Vogue*. House music and a weekly Brazilian party are among the many attractions.... *Tel 305/674–7870. 653 Washington Ave., Miami Beach.*

Versailles. Stop in for a cafecito at this Calle Ocho restaurant, which has been visited over the years by political candidates and refugees alike.... *Tel 305/444–0240. 3555 SW 8th St., Miami.*

Virtua Cafe. Virtual-reality helmets sit side by side with more traditional saloon pleasures, such as a good-looking clientele and a lively bar.... *Tel 305/532–0234. 1309 Washing-ton Ave., Miami Beach.*

West End. Lugubrious gay bar that is acceptable if you don't feel like crossing town for a better one.... *Tel 305/538–9378. 942 Lincoln Rd., Miami Beach.*

Wet Willie's. Grain-alcohol slushies, a great upper terrace with a view of Ocean Drive, plus the ocean itself make this a loose, fun place to spend an evening, but don't make plans for the the rest of the night after a few of Willie's bombshell drinks.... *Tel 305/532–5650. 760 Ocean Dr., Miami Beach.*

the

3

arts

In the 1960s, an entertainment-filled evening in Miami meant paying to see a legendary headliner such as Frank Sinatra, Nat King Cole, or Marlene Dietrich, and then making the rounds to a series of seedier, if ever-more-colorful diversions. And you could forget about Puccini, Ibsen or Tennessee Williams. After all, everyone was here for fun of the more vulgar sort: Nobody wanted to think. But then, inevitably, that started to change. With the number of full-time residents increasing, most of whom demanded a little more variety in their cultural diets, the spectrum of attractions began to grow.

Three decades later, efforts to turn this city into a magnet for the working arts have *begun* to pay off. Most recently, the broad cultural diversity of Miami's citizenry and the influx of a younger, hipper group of residents—many of whom have moved from cultural capitals such as New York and San Francisco—has added momentum to this shift.

The bottom line? Well, Miami is no longer a *total* cultural wasteland awash in nothing but the pleasures of the flesh, the mix and the latest designer threads. Now we have a number of good local theater companies (as well as a few old war-horses that have been here since the dawn of the Fontainebleau era), a duet of locally based symphonic orchestras, and a number of headstrong impresarios who throw caution to the wind and insist that both Miamians and visitors are extremely willing to show up at the most highbrow or innovative performances they can come up with. In addition, the avant-garde nature of South Beach makes it a key place for visiting performance artists of the edgier sort, most of whom are immediately appreciated and roundly applauded just for showing up.

Still, for a city of its size, Miami's arts scene is small and in need of constant nurturing and watchfulness. And though Miami is gradually becoming an industry town for the production of film, music, and television, so far, little of this creative effort has had much impact on the live arts. Nevertheless, just as the quality of hotels, restaurants, and nightlife continues to improve, so too does the quality of available productions, especially during the winter months of high season. Locals are not starved anymore, just a little hungry.

Sources

Though visitors should find more than enough to stimulate them during their stay, they may have to hunt a little to find the finer points of interest. After all, there is no designated "arts district," that one would find in other towns. But a comprehensive guide to happenings around town, from concerts

to films to gallery shows, can be found in the *Miami Herald*'s
Friday "Weekend," and in the free weekly *New Times*, which
appears every Wednesday in red-and-white boxes around
town. The *Herald* may be slightly more stodgy in its entertainment listings, but both papers are remarkably handy. Drop
into **Uncle Sam's Music** (1141 Washington Ave., Miami
Beach) to check on smaller, alternative events.

Getting Tickets

Tickets to major events can be purchased through **Ticketmaster** (tel 305/358–5885). For all-in-one ticket buying—
from concerts to sports events—there are a variety of options,
including **Preferred Travel & Tickets** (tel 305/443–3000),
Ultimate Travel & Entertainment (tel 305/444–8499), and
Global Tickets (tel 800/625–8184). A last-ditch call can
always be made to **Grand Entertainment Services** (tel 305/
358–0908), which boasts "prime seats to sold-out events," and
actually delivers pretty well on that promise.

MIAMI ⟨ THE ARTS

The play's the thing... An institution for more than 40 years, the **Coconut Grove Playhouse,** nestled between the jungle of Main Highway and the frenetic bustle of CocoWalk and Mayfair a few blocks north, began life in the 1920s as a cinema. In the late 1940s, it was transformed into a legitimate theater and went on to host such legendary stars as Tallulah Bankhead (in *A Streetcar Named Desire*), Eartha Kitt (in *Timbuktu*), and Bert Lahr and Tom Ewell (in the pre-New York American premiere of *Waiting for Godot*). Today, it still pulls in big stars, including Liza Minnelli, Joel Grey, and Bea Arthur, in a mix of comedies, dramas, and musicals. The seasons can be uneven, however, and the house often panders to a less-elevated commercial sensibility. Fashioned like a Broadway theater, the Playhouse's main house has a luxurious auditorium and ornate detailing. It's here that you'll see the off-Broadway hits, the pre-Broadway musicals, or television-esque comedies with the likes of Jerry Stiller, Len Cariou, and Pia Zadora. A second, smaller stage presents more innovative work, including plays that reflect the lifestyles of the city's Latin community. The experience of seeing a show here is wonderful, but pick carefully—the Playhouse often features lackluster productions carved out of standard formulas. Still, the technical quality is top-drawer, and each season includes at least one scintillating production. Roaring through town every season, the blockbuster **Greater Miami Broadway Series** brings big-budget stars and glitter to Dade, Broward, and Palm Beach counties, usually the pick of the most recent New York season (recently, *Hello, Dolly!* with Carol Channing, *Kiss of the*

Spider Woman with Chita Rivera, *Blood Brothers* with Petula Clark, and the omnipresent *The Phantom of the Opera*). The current venue of choice for these road shows is the **Jackie Gleason Theatre of the Performing Arts (TOPA)**, where the Great One filmed his 1960s television series; TOPA lies in happy proximity to the restaurants and clubs of South Beach. With Miami's new performing arts center opening downtown in 1997, TOPA may get some competition.

One of the best auditoriums in town, offering perfect sight lines from sharply rising seats, is the **Colony Theatre**, another deco gem that began life as a deluxe cinema during Hollywood's Golden Age. Once one of the prime film houses on Lincoln Road, the reconstructed and refurbished Colony (the plush carpeting is a knockoff of Radio City Music Hall's famous red-and-white floor covering) now hosts a variety of theatrical productions, as well as music and dance concerts. Some of the in-your-face performance pieces presented here in recent years seem jarringly out of place amidst the posh decor. Downtown Miami's **Gusman Center for the Performing Arts**, the baroque jewel in the city's crown, is even more splendid. All gilt and plush, the Gusman is yet another theater that began life as a movie palace. Its ceiling, filled with a zillion twinkling stars, gives the audience the illusion of sitting under a night sky. In fact, if you get bored with the show, you can always stare at the ceiling. Host to a number of big touring companies, the Gusman recently presented the Florida premiere of *Angels in America*, to rave reviews. Finally, in Coral Gables, you'll find the **Actors' Playhouse,** which presents a repertoire of old and brassy new shows, recently relocated to the venerable and majestic **Miracle Theatre,** on Miracle Mile.

There are no small theaters... On Miami Beach's Lincoln Road, the tiny, independent **Area Stage** has gained a reputation for provocative contemporary works. The space is so intimate that during some shows the actors are practically sitting in your lap, but that just adds to the vitality of the productions. Afterwards you can stuff your face at one or more of the myriad alfresco cafes that line the street. Notwithstanding its name, the **Florida**

Shakespeare Theatre produces more than just the Bard. Although a recent season presented *Julius Caesar* and *Anthony and Cleopatra*, their almost blindingly eclectic schedule also included John Guare's *Six Degrees of Separation*, Eugene O'Neill's *The Hairy Ape*, and *You're a Good Man, Charlie Brown!* The season is presented at Coral Gables' elegant **Biltmore Hotel**, the stunning Med Rev structure that defined Florida in the roaring twenties. The company is still rather low-key, but good things are expected. **The University of Miami's Ring Theatre** is perhaps the area's leading venue for aspiring student actors. Light-hearted and serious works are performed well, right on the campus; the new **Jerry Herman Theatre**, named after the alumnus and Broadway composer, offers state-of-the-art facilities. Lastly, Coral Gables' tiny **New Theatre** lures increasing numbers of discriminating theatergoers to its out-of-the-way location, with season after season of consistently winning dramas, comedies, and cabaret.

Classical sounds... The state of classical music has improved tremendously since local impresario Judy Drucker first began presenting intimate concerts in her synagogue more than 25 years ago. Nowadays grande dame Judy's **Concert Association of Florida** brings the world's most luminous names in longhair music to venues throughout the region. Itzhak Perlman, Kathleen Battle, Van Cliburn, Mikhail Baryshnikov, Zubin Mehta, and the Israeli Philharmonic—all have appeared under Drucker's aegis. In the mid-nineties, she may have scored her biggest coup of all when she presented Luciano Pavarotti, literally singing on the beach with full orchestra, to an audience of thousands. But immense orchestras and solo virtuosos are only the tip of the musical iceberg. Lately she has moved into dance: Twyla Tharp's dancers and Mikhail Baryshnikov's White Oak Project are two of La Drucker's recent conquests. CAF's concerts usually land at the Dade County Auditorium downtown or Jackie Gleason's TOPA in Miami Beach. South Florida's own symphony orchestra, the **Florida Philharmonic**, is a first-class regional orchestra that's popularly accepted, critically tolerated, but losing money like so many arts organizations in these tight fiscal times. They perform the full range of classics from Bach to Stravinsky and beyond, under the baton of conductor James Judd, with a number of guest appearances by leading soloists every season. Concerts by the Philharmonic's extremely popular stepchild, its pops orchestra, are directed by Peter Nero. Both orchestras usually play at the downtown Gusman Center, though they've been known to set up their music stands at other venues around town, as well as in Fort Lauderdale and Palm Beach.

Miami Beach is the lab for an extremely adventurous musical experiment: Star conductor Michael Tilson Thomas' **New World Symphony** is an organization composed entirely of young musicians, fresh from training. Since Tilson Thomas is committed to modern music, these concerts are usually the most avant-garde in town (one very well-received recent concert combined Mozart with Barber, Bernstein, and Steve Reich). Finally, the **Florida Grand Opera**, a recent merger of the Miami and Fort Lauderdale opera companies, annually presents four grand operas with full orchestration, good international voices, and impressive-to-stunning production values. Really. Their repertoire runs the gamut from Handel to Gershwin.

Congregational sounds... Since the Miami musical scene has expanded, fewer churches and temples offer top-flight musical performances outside of their services. One shining example, however, is Kendall's **Temple Beth Am**, which consistently engages renowned names in classical piano and violin to regale the cognoscenti with their lyrical flights. In addition, the building, itself, is an exceptional place to see a performer, with wonderful sight lines and brilliant acoustics.

Men in tights... Dade County hosts one of the country's foremost companies: Edward Villella's **Miami City Ballet (MCB)**. A protégé of the late George Balanchine at the New York City Ballet, Villella has been determined to carry on his mentor's legacy and, so far, he's been delivering. Many of the MCB's productions revive old Balanchine works such as *Jewels*, a sixties effort from the master that was greeted with much acclaim by nineties critics and audiences. And when this troupe took its show on the road a while back, Villella's re-creation of *Western Symphony* wowed Washington, D.C.'s Kennedy Center

MIAMI ⟨ THE ARTS

swells. It's not just a Balanchine fan club, though: Other choreographers are also given their due, from Jimmy Gamonet de los Heros to Agnes de Mille. A more modest but nonetheless noteworthy organization is the **Performing Arts Network (PAN)**, an umbrella group that presents dance, drama, and musical events in its Miami Beach space, off Lincoln Road. One member company is the Ballet Flamenco La Rosa, a fiery troupe that has attracted attention with its traditional Latin choreography. Other local modern dance talents, such as the Momentum Dance Company and Freddick Bratcher and Company, are also featured.

Promoters and impresarios... Performance artists do indeed come to Miami, often under the aegis of the **Miami Light Project.** One of the pioneers of the South Beach renewal, the Miami Light Project brings to town performers no one else would book here, such as Spalding Gray, avant-garde performer Diamanda Galas, and the Los Angeles Chicano comedy trio Culture Clash, who were commissioned to create an original piece focusing on Miami's racial mix. Most artists are showcased at Miami Beach's Colony Theatre. Another innovative group is the **Cultura Del Lobo**, a division of Miami-Dade Community College that presents adventurous contemporary programs such as Odadaa, a troupe of musicians and dancers from Ghana. The main event of their season is the highly regarded Subtropics Music Festival, a springtime roundup of emerging artists and renowned composers from around the world, including experimental music, dance, and multimedia at various venues around town. Though Miami doesn't really host an indigenous performance-art culture, there are a few local performers—chiefly through J. C. Carroll's Art Act—who stage one or two evenings of monologues and showcases, often at the Colony Theater on Lincoln Road.

Stars and planets... The **Miami Space Transit Planetarium**, like many across the country, offers Friday and Saturday night laser light shows to the music of Pink Floyd, The Beatles, and Led Zeppelin. Check times for your musical preference. The animated sequences and laser lights *are* truly spectacular. In addi-

tion, a more sober evening discussion/lecture regarding
the constellations takes place before the music gets
rocking.

The silver screen... Though some of the latest films
from Hollywood and elsewhere in the world take a
while to reach Miami—about as long as they take to get
to Omaha—the city does host one of the country's most
sparkling cinematic hullabaloos. Every February, the
Miami Film Festival presents two frenetic weeks of
premieres, parties, celebrities, and press. Born from
modest origins about ten years ago, the event sky-
rocketed to fame largely because of its American premieres of a number of films by Pedro Almodóvar, the
Spanish director whose campy flights entranced Miami.
The hoopla surrounding the festival now resembles a
circus, with stars, galas, and glamour galore. Though it
showcases new movies from around the world, the festival has gained attention for its promotion of Hispanic-
themed movies from the United States, as well as exciting Latin work from Central and South America and
Spain. Movies like *The Mambo Kings* and *Miami
Rhapsody* made their debuts at this festival before spinning into oblivion in the nation's octoplexes. Though
these screenings are usually sellouts—people flock to
catch a glimpse of their favorite film stars and glit-
terati—it is possible to get tickets if you call three or
four months in advance. The rest of the year, however,
you'll have to be content with a couple of small art-film
houses such as the **Alliance** on South Beach's Lincoln
Road, a beautiful, cloistered gem entered through a
wonderful tropical underbrush. The finest in European
and American art cinema is exclusively screened here, in
an intimate setting awash with blasé chic. There's also
the cozy **Astor** in Coral Gables. Their programming
isn't wildly adventurous, but at least it's not first-run,
big-studio dreck. For that you'll have to head over to
the mallplex that is widely regarded as one of Miami's
most comfortable cinemas: Coconut Grove's **Cocowalk**
has 16 screens worth of the finest from Hollywood,
New York, and abroad. In fact, this may be the quintessential mall cinema, complete with plush chairs, yummy
concessions, and a screenland mood. In addition, view-
ers are surrounded by a wide variety of stores and

MIAMI ☽ THE ARTS

restaurants, making going to the movies a complete evening's entertainment. Meanwhile, a far more elegant alternative is the **Bay Harbor Four Theaters**, located discreetly on a chain of islands stretching west from Bal Harbour. Though no longer a single-screen house, the current theater is soundproofed and sumptuously decorated. The spiral staircase is great fun, too—like some mad Busby Berkeley set piece. It's the preferred choice for mainstream film connoisseurs.

Latin floor shows... The great age of the nightclub show—so much a part of Miami and Havana in the 1950s—lives on at select clubs. At many of these spots you can dine, drink, see the show, and dance the night away all at one venue. One particularly mad and wacky throwback is the **Club Tropigala**, in Miami Beach's Fontainebleau Hilton, which showcases mid-century-style glittering chorines bedecked with feathered headdresses. Dinner, dancing, drinks, showgirls, music, laughs, more drinks, more dancing—it's the Rat Pack all over again. Arguably the greatest souvenir from the glory days of old Havana, **Les Violins**, is a riotous spectacle. Operated by a venerable professional nightclub family from Cuba, this spot on Biscayne Boulevard is reviving traditions straight from the lore of old Havana. The most glamorous ladies and their dapper gents order Cuban delicacies, fine wines, and stiff drinks; take in the shows; and then dance till the wee hours to sultry Latin bands. Finally, a more up-to-date Cuban experience: At **Centro Vasco**, on Little Havana's Calle Ocho, the vibrant performances of Albita Rodriguez and her band (they fled Cuba in 1993) caused an electric stir like none Miami had seen for years. Now part of Gloria and Emilio Estefan's talent stable, Rodriguez has moved on, but amazing Cuban singers and musicians still perform in what would be an authentic Cuban nightclub setting—if Cuba still had nightclubs. And if you still want to see Rodriguez, she and her band can be seen on Thursdays and Sundays at **Yuca**, a sublimely chic nouvelle Latin restaurant on Miami Beach's Lincoln Road (see Late Night Dining). They also do occasional performances at other venues around town, including the hot club, Liquid. (See The Club Scene).

Concert venues... When gargantuan acts like Billy Joel, Elton John, or the Rolling Stones come to town, they usually opt, naturally enough, for the biggest possible venue: **Joe Robbie Stadium**, which accommodates about 50,000. Quirkier performers like David Byrne or Laurie Anderson opt for downtown's rococo **Gusman Center for the Performing Arts**, where a twinkling starlit ceiling adds a great deal more charm to the proceedings. Other performers of various ilk are booked into smaller venues like the **Colony Theatre** or the **Jackie Gleason Theatre of the Performing Arts**, both in Miami Beach.

MIAMI ☾ THE ARTS

The Index

Actors' Playhouse. This thoroughly professional company mixes sparkling favorites from the past with newer works.... *Tel 305/444–9293. 280 Miracle Mile, Coral Gables.*

Alliance. Hidden away cinema showing independent and foreign films.... *Tel 305/531–8504. 927 Lincoln Rd., Miami Beach.*

Area Stage. Not unlike a small house in New York's downtown scene, this local favorite challenges audiences with mind-expanding contemporary works.... *Tel 305/673–8002. 645 Lincoln Rd., Miami Beach.*

Astor. Coral Gables' small art film house.... *Tel 305/443–6777. 4120 Laguna St., Coral Gables.*

Bay Harbor Four Theaters. A classy, older venue that they've managed to slice up into a fourplex, without sacrificing too much of the charm... *Tel 305/866–2441. 1170 King Concourse, Bay Harbour Island.*

Centro Vasco. Although the decor borders on kitsch, this family-operated Little Havana club is the real Cuban item, full of the original emigres who fled Castro's revolution and talented—often more recently arrived—performers from the homeland. Fast-rising Albita Rodriguez made her first splash in Miami here.... *Tel 305/643–9626. 2235 SW 8th St., Miami.*

Club Tropigala. A mad Miami romp, Club Tropigala presents an old-Havana floor show in an over-the-top setting. Loud, gaudy, memorable.... *Tel 305/672–7469. 4441 Collins Ave., Fontainebleau Hilton, Miami Beach. Open Thur–Sun.*

Coconut Grove Playhouse. The most venerable and respected of Miami's theaters.... *Tel 305/442–2662. 3500 Main Highway, Coconut Grove.*

Cocowalk. Just like the mall at home, only bigger and plusher, with 16 screens of Hollywood blockbuster fun.... *Tel 305/ 448–6641. 3015 Grand Ave., Miami.*

Colony Theatre. This deco gem on Miami Beach now hosts a variety of theatrical productions, as well as concerts and dance performances.... *Tel 305/674–1026. 1040 Lincoln Rd., Miami Beach.*

Concert Association of Florida. Premier impresario Judy Drucker brings the greatest names in classical music and dance to Miami's shores. Concerts are either at the Dade County Auditorium or the Jackie Gleason Theatre of the Performing Arts.... *Tel 305/532–3491. 555 17th St., Miami Beach.*

Cultura Del Lobo. This division of Miami-Dade Community College presents contemporary international music, dance, and art events. Their annual Subtropics Music Festival is held in the spring on the college's Wolfson campus.... *Tel 305/237–3010. 300 NE 2nd Ave., Ste. 1401, Miami.*

Dade County Auditorium. Downtown venue for concerts and dance.... *Tel 305/545–3395. 2901 Flagler St., Miami.*

Florida Grand Opera. The opera companies of Miami and Fort Lauderdale recently combined their forces to present four truly grand productions a year. Performances are usually staged at the Dade County Auditorium.... *Tel 305/854– 1643. 1200 Coral Way, Miami.*

Florida Philharmonic. Miami's resident symphonic orchestra performs the classical war-horses at either the Gusman Center or the Jackie Gleason Theatre of the Performing Arts. Peter Nero presides over pops orchestra concerts.... *Tel 305/577–0444. 169 E. Flagler St., Ste. 1534, Miami.*

Florida Shakespeare Theatre. With a spanking-new theater in the Biltmore Hotel and an outdoor theater soon to open, this company is rapidly growing. While the season's highlight is the Shakespeare Festival in the early spring, there are additional plays scattered throughout the year.... *Tel 305/446–1116. 1200 Anastasia Ave., Coral Gables.*

Greater Miami Broadway Series. The latest hits of the New York season are brought to Miami, thanks to this organization. Stars, glitter, and splash are the rules of these road shows. Productions are usually staged at the Jackie Gleason Theatre of the Performing Arts (see below).... *Tel 305/379–2700. One Bayfront Plaza, 100 S. Biscayne Blvd., Ste. 1200, Miami.*

Gusman Center for the Performing Arts. A gilded gem of an old movie house, the Gusman is home to major touring companies.... *Tel 305/374–8762. 174 E. Flagler St., Miami.*

Jackie Gleason Theatre of the Performing Arts. This large theater is where the Great One used to film his television show in the sixties.... *Tel 305/673–7300. 1700 Washington Ave., Miami Beach.*

Miami City Ballet. The brainchild of celebrated Balanchine protégé Edward Villella, the Miami City Ballet usually performs at the Dade County Auditorium or Jackie Gleason Theatre of the Performing Arts.... *Tel 305/532–4880. 905 Lincoln Rd., Miami Beach. October–May.*

The Miami Film Festival. This annual February frolic is fast becoming one of the country's finest celebrations of film. Screenings are held at the Gusman Center for the Performing Arts.... *Tel 305/377–3456. 444 Brickell Ave., Miami.*

Miami Light Project. This organization's lineup of cutting-edge (and in some cases, wacky) musicians, dancers, and performance artists have met with tremendous acclaim. Most performances are at the Colony Theatre.... *Tel 305/865–8477. Box 402501, Miami Beach.*

Miami Space Transit Planetarium. From sleep-inducing lectures on astronomy to psychedelic Pink Floyd laser shows, this place has it all.... *Tel 305/854–2222. 3280 S. Miami Ave., Coconut Grove.*

MIAMI ⟨ THE ARTS

New Theatre. Tucked away on a side street in Coral Gables, this small theater has garnered critical acclaim in recent years for its innovative musical and dramatic productions.... *Tel 305/443–5909. 65 Almeria Ave., Coral Gables.*

New World Symphony. International star conductor Michael Tilson Thomas leads recent graduates of top conservatories in a mostly modern repertoire.... *Tel 305/673–3330. Lincoln Theatre, 541 Lincoln Rd., Miami Beach.*

Performing Arts Network (PAN). A coalition of performing artists and arts organizations, this group presents dance, drama, and musical events.... *Tel 305/672–0552. 555 17th St., Miami Beach.*

Temple Beth Am. Relax to this temple's classical concert series, or take advantage of their programs for the kiddies, in which little ones can learn about such varied topics as jazz or musical instruments.... *Tel 305/667–6667. 5959 N. Kendall Dr., Kendall. No summer performances.*

TOPA. See **Jackie Gleason Theatre of the Performing Arts.**

University of Miami's Ring Theatre. Hosts productions by both amateur students and professionals from outside the university.... *Tel 305/284–3355. 1380 Miller Dr., Coral Gables.*

Les Violins. Showgirls, rum cocktails, and Cuban delicacies abound. Ricky Ricardo, eat your heart out... *Tel 305/371–8668. 1751 Biscayne Blvd., Miami.*

spo

rts 4

It's nearly 6am on Ocean Drive. A statuesque Elle MacPherson type in a G-string bikini blades right by an even taller drag queen, sans heels and makeup, jogging in gold lamé sweats. That image—on tap at almost any hour in South Beach—epitomizes the way sports, fashion, and nightlife have crazily intersected in Miami, where athleticism practically equals eroticism... or at least invites shameless voyeurism. The 'tude is so extreme that at certain gyms anyone whose body fat exceeds 10 percent receives a "why bother?" look more withering and dismissive than any club doorman's. The body beautiful—and exposed—is the Miami credo. Remember, this is the town that redefined casual chic; in other words, the less you can get away with wearing, the better. Obviously, sailing, swimming, windsurfing, Jet Skiing, surfing, and waterskiing are all pursued at least until that last sliver of light around eight o'clock, with the Atlantic Ocean, Key Biscayne and the miles of waterways that lace through the city as the playing fields. But folks also take to terra firma: runners, bladers, skateboarders, and bikers all cruise under the lights of South Beach and even the Grove. Meanwhile lit courts and fields are buzzing with people playing basketball, handball, street hockey, and even cricket.

This fanatic hauteur even extends to the local pro and college teams. *Oye mami,* is this ever a sports town. Fans are plentiful and plenty rabid—which means last-minute tickets are easier to get for the latest Madonna concert than when the home teams are in action. Miamians are sports-starved. For years the only major league game in town was the Miami Dolphins, five-time Super Bowl champs and unquestionably the kingfish in South Florida. For years they were guided by Don Shula, the "winningest" coach in NFL history and still a demigod in this town. But the installation of former University of Miami and Dallas Cowboys head coach Jimmy Johnson at the Dolphins' helm (see "Pigskin," below) bodes well for the team's future success.

But the hottest tickets in town may well be for the Heat, Miami's first NBA franchise. Their record thus far could hardly be called stellar, but who cares when tabloid royals the likes of Melanie Griffith are vying for those seats at center court? Besides, the arrival of slick coach Pat Riley, lured with megabucks after storied stints in Los Angeles and New York, has given new life to both Heat fans and local hair-mousse vendors.

Until 1993, the Atlanta Braves were the closest thing Floridians had to a professional "field of dreams," but that all changed with the advent of the uneven but much loved Florida Marlins. The 1994 strike put a damper on fan loyalty, and owner Wayne Huizenga (of Blockbuster Video fame) has pumped nearly $30 million into free-agent signings the last couple of years; so far your video dollars have bought the sexiest uniforms in baseball (turquoise-and-white numbers) but no pennants, with none in the foreseeable future.

Rounding out the four corners of the sports world are the Florida Panthers, the NHL hockey team that often counts as many Canadians among its fans as Miamians. The Panthers have developed into a winning team, however, and contrary to expectations, hell has not yet frozen over.

Still, the most entertaining game in town may well be watching the continual flux (and flex) of Miami's satin-and-silk jockstrap culture. And you'd be surprised how many calories you can burn swiveling your head back and forth.

Getting Tickets

Surprise, surprise—the primary source for tickets to major events is **Ticketmaster** (tel 305/358–5885). For sports events, there are a variety of other options, including **Preferred Travel & Tickets** (tel 305/443–3000), **Ultimate Travel & Entertainment** (tel 305/444–8499), and **Global Tickets** (tel 800/625–8184). If the game you want to see is sold out, you might be able to score tickets with a call to **Grand Entertainment Services** (tel 305/439–6565), which will often be able to find you good seats, albeit for a price.

The Lowdown

Where to watch

Pigskin... Miami's big fish and pro football team, the **Dolphins,** play at Joe Robbie Stadium (tel 305/620–2578; 2269 N.W. 199th St., Miami). This immense concrete stadium, just a 30-minute trek from downtown, is loyally bedecked in the turquoise-and-orange team colors. The stadium sits on the outskirts of Dade County, a first down away from Broward County. The "Fins," as the team is called, are storied Super Bowl champs, but it's been over twenty years, and hometown fans (Dol-fans) are especially loyal to former longtime Fin coach Don Shula, now that he has finally gotten the message and retired. Never again to stand on the sidelines barking orders to quarterback Dan Marino—a local favorite sports celebrity (with an eponymous sports bar in Coconut Grove; see The Bar Scene)—Shula called it quits with the Dolphins in late 1995 and his replacement, former University of Miami head coach Jimmy Johnson, shows his stuff, starting with the 1996 season. Tickets to the games get sold quickly, even though the stadium seats some 50,000. Meanwhile, on the college side are the University of Miami Hurricanes, perennial contenders for the number-one ranking, who have taken over the Orange Bowl, former home of their grown-up compatriots, the Dolphins. It's hard to say which of these two teams elicits greater support from local football fans, but Hurricanes games are right up there as the biggest events in Miami. The off-the-field exploits of these "bad boys" of college football are as heavily exploited in the local media as their on-the-field success (tel 800/GO-CANES; 1501 NW 3rd St., Miami). Check their schedule to see if you can catch one of the occasional night games during their season.

Peanuts and Cracker Jack... When the Dolphins leave at season's end, the **Marlins** swim in to Joe Robbie Stadium (tel 305/620–2578; 2269 NW 199th St., Miami). In the major leagues we're still minnows, competing against the kingfish. The Marlins made their first major league splash on April 5, 1993, and ever since, the team has been trying to make a name for itself nationally. Locally they are loved, and crowds at the games—nearly all of which take place at night, after the day's rain shower has lessened the humidity a bit—run the range from dads with sons to clumps of sports yuppies sporting their stylin' Marlins baseball caps.

Slapshots... Since this fledgling pro hockey franchise's debut was only three years ago, you'd imagine the **Panthers** might have a slow start—not! These guys are on the move, fast forward. Having already gotten a Stanley Cup final under their belts, they have established a credible name for themselves, and a loyal following, in record time. (The games can get rowdy, loud, and rough. And we're not even talking about the players—that's just the cheering and jeering fans; Sometimes they look more active than the players butting heads on the ice or slipping on the rubber rats the fans throw to show their support.) The Panthers prowl, bleed, shove, and break teeth at the **Miami Arena** (tel 305/530–4400; 721 NW 1st Ave., Miami). Local trivia: The Panthers have spawned a rat-flinging mania among local hockey fans. The rat craze started when Panther player Scott Mellanby killed a locker-room rat with a hockey stick, then scored two goals. Since then, the games have been rattled with rat-a-tat-rats at the arena, where temps are cool, and to-go cups of beer are hoisted with each point scored. Bring a sweater and a rubber rat.

Hoop dreams... The city's NBA basketball team, the **Miami Heat** plays at the **Miami Arena** (tel 305/530–4400; 721 NW First Ave., Miami). When suave and debonair Pat Riley was imported to Miami a couple of years ago as the team's coach, the local glitz quotient of the game went way up. Miami resident Madonna and assorted groovy gal pals have been spotted at Heat games, as well as thousands of others who come to see Alonzo Mourning and the rest of the long-legged crew thunder down the court.

Smaller balls... Finally, thanks in no small part to its extraordinary atmospheric conditions, Miami's International Tennis Center is host to a prestigious annual tennis tournament. The **Lipton Tennis Classic** (tel 305/446-2200; 7300 Crandon Boulevard., Key Biscayne; call for match schedule) brings mobs of eager fans to the beautiful banks of Key Biscayne each spring to watch major and minor stars from the racquet world battle under the lights for those endorsement dollars.

Playing the puppies... Although Hialeah Race Track, with its salmon-pink flamingos, fountains and majestic staircases is sadly closed at night, if you're sorely in need of some action, just cross town to watch the pooches race at **Flagler Greyhound Track** (tel 305/649-3000; NW 37th Ave. and 7th St., Miami). It's not as rich in history or as fancy as its Hialeah counterpart, but locals pour into this place. Racing starts at 7:30pm and runs through 11. Expect Cuban businessmen puffing cigars, shorts-clad middle-aged fellas trying to make a buck, and groups of young Latinos swapping tips and laughs.

Where to play

Biking... Because there's such a hustling and bustling nightlife in Miami, there aren't many safe places to cycle without getting honked at (maybe that's why God invented Walkmans). But that doesn't stop in-the-know natives who aren't simply *too* cool from using two wheels to make their nocturnal rounds. At least you aren't stuck *in* those honking, bumper-to-bumper cars. Some folks pedal on the boardwalk behind the grand canyon of hotels and condos, on Miami Beach (21st to 47th streets), even though signs say it is forbidden. The boardwalk is well-lit and well-traveled at night. If you get tired, you can always stop at the Fontainebleau Hilton and listen to live lounge bands serenade hotel guests with music from the islands. A concrete bike path—semilit at night by nearby traffic—that also doubles as a jogging and skating trail wends around **Crandon Beach Park** (tel 305/361–7385; 4000 Crandon Blvd., Key Biscayne), near Key Biscayne. The park was touted by national travel mags as one of the country's best beaches by day. While you're on Key Biscayne, trek the 12 miles of trails that connect the Key Biscayne toll plaza at the Rickenbacker Causeway to Bill Baggs Cape Florida State Recreation Area. The Venetian Islands, a string of six islands laced from Miami to Miami Beach, also provide good turf to trek on two wheels. For brochures about biking in Dade County, call the **Dade County Bicycle and Pedestrian Program** (tel 305/375–4507).

Even though Miami stays up just about as late as any city in the country, it's hard to find a place to rent a two-wheeler at night, so get your wheels before nightfall. In the heart of South Beach, just a spit away from the cafes, clubs, and beach, **Gary's Mega Cycle** (tel 305/534–3306; 1261 Washington Ave., Miami Beach; open until 7pm) rents a kaleidoscope of bikes, from mountain to tenspeeds, for $5 an hour or $15 a day. Cyclers can keep the bikes overnight, but they'll have to beat it back to the shop to return them by 10am.

Ice capades... The only game in town for ice skating is the **Miami Ice Arena** (tel 305/940–8222; 14770 Biscayne Blvd., North Miami Beach; open until 10pm). Mostly the haunt of teenagers, the rink is aswirl on weekend nights with Nancy Kerrigan wannabes performing their figure eights, and the little Tonya Hardings who love to knock them down. Bring a sweater and $5 for entry (that covers the cost of skate rental, too).

Jai alai... Wanna jai alai? Translated from Basque (the Spanish hill country where the game originated), the name means "merry festival." Learning to play the sport, tagged as the world's fastest game, can be fun, but it will take patience, persistence, and concentration. And you *will* get a workout. Jai alai is similar to racquetball and other court games—you catch the ball in the air with a *cesta* (baskets attached to a leather glove that is tied onto the hand with a *cinta*, or string), and after one bounce

MIAMI ☽ SPORTS

you hurl it back toward the front wall. You can hit the side wall first and also play off the back wall. In Miami, if you want to watch the pros (as well as bet on them) there's **Miami Jai Alai** (tel 305/633–6400; 3500 NW 37th Ave., Miami; open until midnight). Neophytes and enthusiasts can then try it out at **North Miami Amateur Jai Alai** (tel 305/944–8217; 1935 NE 150th St., North Miami; open until 10pm), with hourly court rentals at $4 per person.

On the run... Miami doesn't have huge hills to tackle, which means it's great for beginning runners and long-distance walkers, especially at night when the heat isn't on. The elevated, wooden **boardwalk** that hugs the beachside, behind the Miami Beach hotels and condos from 21st to 47th streets, gives runners a long stretch of track to trek. Power walkers command the scene here, along with parents strollering tykes who can't sleep or stay in during the heat of the day, skaters, and the Geritol generation. **South Pointe Park**'s (tel 305/673–7730; southern tip of Miami Beach) jogging trail winds through 17 waterfront acres bordering Government Cut. If you run Friday evenings between 5 and 7, you'll catch the majestic sight of cruise ships heading out of the channel into the Atlantic. The park also has a help-yourself exercise program marked with instructional signs. Just look for the wooden exercise equipment scattered along the jogging trail. Nearby **Bayshore Golf Course** (tel 305/532–3550; 2301 Alton Rd., Miami Beach) has a paved bike path that wraps around the golf course. The best time to run here is sunset, as the caddies putter their way back to the clubhouse and the bold colors of the sky are reflected in the ponds and lakes. You'll see the cars zipping by on the roadways, but you'll feel far away. On the mainland, walkers and joggers cram **South Bayshore Drive** between Miami and Coconut Grove. There's a path for jogging, walking, and bicycling.

Pickup places... For roller hockey, or what some call in-line or ballistic hockey, an empty parking lot seems to be a skater's cul-de-sac. The lot across from the **Miami Beach Convention Center** (tel 305/673–7311; 1901 Convention Center Dr., Miami Beach) is a haven for hotshot skaters with hockey sticks. On weekday evenings, especially Wednesdays and Thursdays, catch them roll and rock in the parking lot. For hoops, **the courts at Flamingo Park** (12th St. and Meridian Ave.) buzz with kids romping way past park hours (the park is supposedly closed from midnight to 5am). Near the hoops are the handball courts, where transplanted New York snowbirds smash small blue balls deep into the night.

Rack 'em up... Pool players rack up their games all around the city at night. Chicks who like other chicks, and the men who love them (it gets complicated, especially without Sally Jessy to sort it all out)) shoot some pool at **West End** (tel 305/538–9378; 942 Lincoln Rd., Miami Beach). There are only two pool tables, but there's never really a crowd. Mostly the barflies simply hover, watching the gals and their pals shoot. Each game is a buck, and West End is open until 5am. **The Sterling Club Billiards** (tel 305/531–2114; 1242 Washington Ave., Miami Beach; $9 per hour) has rows and rows of slick green pool tables with wooden frames. Purple neon signs cast an otherworldly glow on the patrons. Local Xers hang out here, as well as young clubby dressed-up couples looking for a break from the chaotic South Beach nights. In North Dade, **Broadway Billiards** (tel 305/935–6600; 17813 Biscayne Blvd., North Miami) serves a yup crowd almost every night. It has a reputation as a singles place, where after-work types loosen their ties and make wagers over games of eight-ball. The place charges each player $4.50 for each hour of play.

Blading... Whip and weave among brawny, bare-chested men, and women in thongs and little else, on **South Beach's beachfront sidewalk, running from Fifth through 16th streets.** This waterside strip that parallels mondo chic **Ocean Drive** is the best concrete ribbon to roll on, but be careful of two-wheelers and walkers. It can look like a war of wheels out there, as everyone vies to glide alongside the sand. To move away from the masses, hop on the **Venetian Islands**, a string of islands smack in the middle of downtown Miami and South Beach, and connected by little drawbridges. The turf is flat, with lots of room for cars and bladers. Only locals tend to use the

MIAMI ⟨ SPORTS

roadway, so traffic doesn't snarl, unless one of the bridges opens up. As you sweep your legs left and right, check out the majestic views of downtown—what color is I. M. Pei's NationsBank tower tonight?—and the water. Die-hard bladers live by the **Key Biscayne paths**, with thigh-sculpting terrain that forces skaters to navigate the arch of the bridge linking the Key to the mainland. You can roll for miles along the water by day or night. Just dump your car in one of the lots parallel to the road shoulders and get out there.

Amateur skaters looking for a good pair of skates can roll into **Fritz Skate Shops** (tel 305/532-1954; 117 5th St. or 726 Lincoln Rd, Miami Beach). Customers can rent skates—$8 an hour, $15 for overnight (6pm to noon the next day) or $24 for a full day (10am to 8pm, with the stores closing at 10pm on weekends)—and return them at either store. Those who decide to make in-line skating a daily habit may purchase Rollerblade or K2 skates in all sizes—prices range from $100 to $350.

Bowling... When the going gets tough, the tough go bowling, even in the dawn hours. To the south, there's **Don Carter's Kendall Lanes** (tel 305/385–6160; 13600 N. Kendall Dr., Miami; $3.15 per person per game), a bowling alley that looks like a shopping mall jammed with kids, teens, and families. The lanes are open 24 hours daily, and they charge $1.75 extra to rent those goofy shoes. With 72 lanes to spare or strike from, there's rarely a wait, and the place is always jumping. To the north, there's **Cloverleaf Lanes** (tel 305/652–4197; 17601 NW 2nd Ave., Miami; open until midnight; $3.15 per person per game), with acres of lanes—50 in all—and electronic scoring.

Swimming... Swimming in the Atlantic Ocean is free and natch any time of the year, day or night, thanks to the always-warm water temps. If you prefer chlorinated fun, most hotels, even the cheesy, small ones, have swimming pools. The grandest of pools belongs to the **Fontainebleau Hilton** (tel 305/538–2000; 4441 Collins Ave., Miami Beach), with a central waterfall and odd curves hugging the amoeba-shaped swimming area, which is open for action round the clock. Though the pool is technically for guests, management tolerates visitors who are low-key. The best entryway for nonguests is via the wooden boardwalk behind the hotel. Walk in as if you are a guest, and no one will be the wiser. Lap swimmers willing to finish up by 7pm might want to try the **University of Miami's** pool on the Coral Gables campus (tel 305/284–3622; 1306 Stanford Drive, Miami). It's home to students whose only use for textbooks is to weigh down their towels. The pool is not officially open to the public, but if you plead out-of-town status and fork over $3, chances are you'll gain admittance. On Miami Beach, the **Scott Rakow Youth Center** (tel 305/673–7767; 2700 Sheridan Ave., Miami Beach) has a big public pool where, for $5, adults can swim laps nightly until 8. (The center is named after a twentysomething Miami Beach police officer who was killed in the line of duty. He was also a coach at the center before becoming a cop.)

Batting cages... So rather than swanning around on skates with a thong in your heart, you just want to hit an old-fashioned fastball? Check out **The Dugout Cages and Athletics,** near ground zero for where Hurricane Andrew hit and now home base for six indoor batting cages (tel 305/252–1858; 18755 South Dixie Hwy., Miami; open until 9pm). Here, baseball buffs can swing by to take a swing at balls that hurtle as fast as 105 miles per hour or as slow as 50. It also gives great value: less than eight cents a pitch for a minimum of twenty.

Up to par... Florida is home to more than 1,000 green golf courses, and Miami has its share of holes. The best for nighttime fun belong to the miniature golf houses, where the fake green grass rules. **Cloverleaf Mini Golf and Game Room** (tel 305/947–1211; 150 NW 167th St., Miami; open until midnight Mon–Fri, until 2am Sat–Sun; $3 per round) offers a wacky, 18-hole course of King Tut pyramids, American homes, and rough green turf to thwack the ball on. At the other end of town is **Malibu Grand Prix** (tel 305/266–2100; 7775 NW 8th St., Miami; open until 10pm on weekdays, until midnight on weekends and throughout summer; prices vary depending on activity), a local teen hangout. Think the *Babysitters Club,* or a freshman year *Beverly Hills 90210* on a night out: Parents drop off their teens for a few hours of golf-

MIAMI ⏾ SPORTS

ing, giggling, and gossiping. For real green on 18 holes of trees and 350-yard fairways, golfers may want to tee off at **Don Shula's Golf Club** (tel 305/821–1150; 7601 NW 154th St., Miami Lakes; open until 11pm; $8 for walkers). Dotted with lakes and sizable sand traps, the longest hole is 150 yards; the shortest, 75. At night, the course is well-lit for twilight tee-offs. And who knows, maybe you'll catch the former Dolphin coach whiling away a few retirement hours.

For gym rats... Most of the grand hotels have their own gyms for guests to build up their pecs and legs. But then there are the gyms of all gyms, where looking good is just as (or more) important as that thing called exercise. Glamour and good looks go hand in hand at **Club Body Tech** (tel 305/674–8222; 1253 Washington Ave., Miami Beach; open until 10:30; $14 for day pass). Body Tech's day pass also includes a high-energy aerobics work out that starts about 7:30pm. Although some may consider the day rate a tad steep at this second-floor gym in the heart of South Beach, taking this class makes it more reasonable. Plus the celeb sightings make the whole experience a cheap thrill. La Madonna, Cindy and her mole, and an array of Baldwin brothers have all been regulars on Body Tech's stair climbers. Pointer: Don't expect this place to announce itself. The entrance is marked only by a small sign affixed to a cinnamon-colored marble facade that's tucked among a typically atypical collection of storefronts. Down the road is **The Gridiron Club** (tel 305/531–4743; 1676 Alton Rd., Miami Beach; open until 11pm Mon–Fri, until 8pm Sat and 6pm Sun), opened a few years ago by former Dolphin defensive back John Bosa. Serious body builders work out here. You hear them grunt, sigh, and strain their veins as they burn their biceps and buns into shape. The latest dance club tunes spin in the background—the $9 day pass includes a night aerobics class that starts at 8pm and wraps up at 9—as the muscled pumpers primp their pretty pecs. The **David Barton Gym** (tel 305/672–2000; 1685 Collins Ave., Miami Beach; open until midnight Mon–Fri, until 9pm Sat–Sun; $15 for day pass, $20 for non-hotel guests) is at the Delano, the hotel of the stars and models, but the public can use the facilities for a fee. The hotel's high ensconcing hedges, the 150-foot sheet of flat blue brimming pool water, and of course, the stars, give this hotel and gym just the right touch of glam to go with the grunt. If you still feel like working out after venturing into this surreal spot, pony up to the pec machine. **The Downtown Athletic Club** (tel 305/358-9988. 200 S. Biscayne Blvd., Miami; day pass is $13, open until 10pm) is a haven for the by-day business crowd looking for a place to pump up and sweat, so you can have your pick of machines and your lane of choice on the club's indoor track or in the cool blue pool at night.

hangi

ng out

5

Buzz-cut pre-teens with
hoop earrings skateboard
through mall parking lots.
Ghostly pale artists
sheathed in black (lace to
leather, take your pick)
slink from one gallery

opening to another. Pony-tailed "photographers" with phony Euro accents and "producers" shackled in gold chains solicit would-be models from their outdoor cafe headquarters. You may not find *quite* the Fellini-esque fashion parade just hanging out in Miami that you do in the bars and clubs, but you will find everyone obeying that RuPaul dictum—"You work that, girl"—with the same abandon. Even the South Beach meter maids pull double duty, ticketing way into the wee hours.

Miami hurtles headlong into the night, as if fueled by endless jolts of the *café Cubano* that locals quaff in quarts throughout the day. Everyone remains on some kind of buzz. This subtropical melting pot is spiced by Miami's extensive cultural and subcultural mix. While the old days of gangster bravura and Jewish ebullience linger still, they are now combined with Latin heat and gay style. Even the most whitebread tourist can't resist the sex appeal. Miami is a voyeur's (and exhibitionist's) delight. So browse in the bookstores, jive in the java joints, or simply stroll the streets. You don't have to go looking for entertainment: it comes straight at you.

Getting Your Bearings

The first thing out-of-towners should realize is that Miami and Miami Beach are separate cities. In Miami Beach the east-west streets are numbered, beginning at the tip of South Beach and progressing northward. The north-south avenues are named. On South Beach—the southernmost end of Miami Beach—the primary commercial avenues are Ocean Drive, Collins, and Washington, and addresses correspond to the numbered streets (i.e., 932 Collins Avenue will be between 9th and 10th streets on Collins).

In Miami, the city grid extends into four quadrants: NW, NE, SE, and SW. Point zero is in downtown Miami on Flagler Street (east-west) and Miami Avenue (north-south). U.S. 1 skirts the eastern edge of Miami and takes on various names: It's Brickell Avenue immediately south of the Miami River downtown, the Dixie Highway when it passes the Rickenbacker Causeway (the east-west road linking Key Biscayne to the mainland). Just north of the Miami River and on into the city of North Miami and up to the county line, U.S. 1 is called Biscayne Boulevard.

Four main causeways arc between Miami and Miami Beach: From south to north, the MacArthur, the Venetian, the Tuttle, and the Broad. The most important one is the

MacArthur (I-395), which feeds onto Fifth Street on Miami Beach; cruise ships line up on the south side at the Port of Miami and palm trees decorate the median. Though it was widened into six lanes in 1995, the MacArthur is still busy on Friday and Saturday nights, as everybody streams over from the mainland to Action Central on South Beach. The Venetian Causeway, which starts in downtown Miami near the *Miami Herald* building, is a two-lane road over a series of residential islands that ends up on 17th street on Miami Beach, the official northern boundary of the Art Deco District. The Venetian costs 50 cents per car, and it's only recommended if you have plenty of time—the half-dozen bridges between the islands are often stuck and the speed limit is 15 mph. The fastest route from Miami to the Beach is the Tuttle (I-195), six lanes of roadway that empties into 41st Street on the beach side. The Broad Causeway's western starting point is on 125th Street on the mainland; it feeds into 96th Street in the village of Bay Harbor Islands on the beach side, and costs 35¢ per car.

You'll need to drive on an expressway or an interstate to reach most of the more interesting sights in Greater Miami, but avoid the high roads during rush hour if you can. SW Eighth Street is an important point of reference—it becomes Calle Ocho, the main street of Little Havana, and then turns into the Tamiami Trail, which runs all the way out to the Everglades and on to Naples. SW 22nd Street is another biggie, leading inland through the heart of Coral Gables. (At various stretches it's also called Coral Way and the Miracle Mile.) Coconut Grove is closer to the water and a bit farther south, where SW 27th Avenue runs into U.S. 1; Main Highway and Grand Avenue are its two chief streets. Of all these neighborhoods, Coral Gables is the most infuriating and difficult to navigate. Streets are curved into obscure angles and street signs are ground-level white stones with names painted in small black letters. (Better to keep the riffraff away, the thinking goes.)

Transportation around Miami is a major hassle unless you have a car. Buses are slow and inconvenient, it's nearly impossible to flag down a taxi on the street, and the MetroRail elevated train system doesn't visit the major points of interest. However, in South Beach you can do it all on foot, calling the occasional cab when your dogs start to bark. Of course, a car will improve your range of options.

The Lowdown

MIAMI ⟨ HANGING OUT

Aerial views... The topography of Greater Miami is flatter than a supermodel's abdomen; you only need a bit of elevation to have the town spread out at your feet like a magic picnic. For the price of a phone call, you can ride and glide on the *Blade Runner*-esque **Metromover** (daily 6am–midnight, 25¢), which slithers like a theme park ride through the Miami skyline. If a little kid isn't hogging one of the big windows, sit down and look out as the high-tech, elevated train slowly slices through the bustling metropolis. From this vantage point, you'll feel like you're looking at Miami through 3-D glasses. Take your air-conditioned ride at sunset: You'll see the big cruise ships docked at the Port of Miami; the last Chalk's seaplane landing at adjacent Government Cut silhouetted against the sun fireballing across the sky; the I. M. Pei–designed NationsBank Tower illuminated in cotton candy colors; and the Freedom Tower, inspired by Seville's graceful Moorish Giralda bell tower. **Hobie Beach,** off the Rickenbacker Causeway near Key Biscayne, offers a glittering vista of Magic City so unreal it resembles a movie set—and of young couples in parked cars, hormones racing. (You'll have to fork over $1 at the bridge toll to enter the Key.)

To see the sunset... Perch yourself atop the Julia Tuttle Causeway (I-195)—connecting Miami to Miami Beach—to see the majestic, sapphire glow over the skyline that screams Kodak moment. (While shutterbugs practically hang off the sides to get the optimum shot and even runners stop to take a breather and take in the sight, be warned that the shoulder is not that wide, and Miamians—especially the geriatric set—drive at a fast clip.) The sun sets pyrotechnically to the west. To the east the condo canyon juts into the Miami Beach skyline. To the south, gawkers can catch the cruise ships gearing up to set sail and to the north is bluish Biscayne Bay's string of little islands which, in 1983, artist Christo draped in flamingo pink.

Walk this way... **Lummus Park,** the 14-block strip of green that runs between the Atlantic Ocean and Ocean Drive on South Beach, is a microcosm of the diverse types that comprise South Beach—leathery geriatrics on park benches kvetching about change, high-altitude models strutting with portfolios in hand, and in-line skaters spiraling on the sidewalks. The park is dotted with benches, a playground for kiddies, and dicey public restrooms that may not always pass a health inspection. Tourists and locals stroll up and down the long pink-and-green-splashed artsy pedestrian **Lincoln Road Mall** (17th St. between Washington Ave. and Alton Rd., Miami Beach), lined with shops, art galleries, cafes, and restaurants. Think of it as a giant sidewalk where skaters and cyclists use pedestrians as slalom gates. Still, it's a somewhat more restrained alternative to the social feeding frenzy of SoBe's Ocean Drive. Folks come to this strip to chill out after dining, drinking, or clubbing, whether it's 6pm, midnight, or 6am. You'll bask in balmy breezes and smell the salty air because the "Road" (as locals call it) is just a few blocks from the beach. If you want to get even closer to the Atlantic, head to the **boardwalk** (from 21st to 53rd sts., behind the condos and hotels), a wooden walkway that hugs the Miami Beach shoreline. Joggers, packs of teenagers, and an international assortment of night worshippers stroll the boardwalk. Farther down, at the tip of South Beach, is **South Pointe Park** (walk-ins free, cars $1). The sound of water lapping against the rocks at Government Cut (the southernmost point) soothes frazzled psyches, especially those that have been battling Miami's endless traffic. Cubans are the dominant group of Miami's many Spanish-speaking communities, and the heart and soul of Cuban Miami is Little Havana, a neighborhood just west of downtown Miami, where a tight-knit enclave of Cuban exiles first settled in the late sixties. The main artery of the neighborhood is **Calle Ocho** (SW 8th St.), a street lined with *cafeterías* (Cuban restaurants) with

MIAMI ⟲ HANGING OUT

streetside coffee windows, cigar-rolling stores (some stay open late on certain nights), and men in guayaberas (loose cotton shirts, also on sale) talking politics and playing dominoes. Most store and street signs are in *español* as well as in English. Behind a menacing set of bars fencing in Maximo Gomez Domino Park (Calle Ocho and 14th St., open until 10pm nightly), earnest groups of men (and men only—an unwritten rule) tamp on their cigarettes, mutter in Spanish, and slide their black-and-white playing pieces across the open-air domino tables. Scenes of old Havana are here, with old men in the park sipping their *tacitas* of Cuban coffee and rowing about whatever.

People watching... In a city full of great- (and extreme-) looking people, one of the finest pleasures is simply to perch somewhere and see what chance will deliver. Miami Beach's **Lincoln Road Mall** is one of the top places for voyeurism. In the earlier part of the evening, pop into **da Leo**, a great, family-run Italian restaurant that happily allows patrons to sit right in the center of the street under the Morris Lapidus–designed, Jetson-esque awnings. And because you're in the center of the street, you're in the center of the action. Later, the **Van Dyke Cafe** (operated by the **News Cafe** owners) stays open until 2am on weekends, midnight on weekdays, and offers another perfect view of the passing pulchritude. Even easier, just find a seat at the central public stopping spot at Lincoln and Euclid. Don't be paranoid if you go to Lincoln Park; passersby stop and stare at other passersby who stroll and stare right back. It's all part of the show. Usually, you'll find a mixed bag of folks on this stretch: Bladers and cyclists check out the scene at night, as well as trendy wannabes and gay muscle men brandishing their biceps. Hordes of people congregate here, making it seem like a human aquarium. Meanwhile, **Ocean Drive** offers an even crazier version of humanity, mostly because these people are all on vacation and are letting their collective hair down. Though they may not be as curiously divine as the locals on Lincoln, they shout and whoop with greater abandon. People Watching Central is the News Cafe, long the perfect outlet for sipping, grazing, and gazing. Coconut Grove's **Cocowalk** (3015 Grand Ave., Coconut Grove) is rife with frat boys, girls in tight shirts, clots of tourists clutching shopping bags, and suits sucking down happy hour specials. The multilevel outdoor mall invites see-and-be-seen-ism (mostly of the collegiate cat-and-mouse variety, especially when you note the lads hanging like monkeys from the balconies on the west end of the complex, hoping for a bird's-eye view of the birds—and not just their wings). See Late Night Dining for more on the above restaurants.

Adult toys... For the horny and humble, looking for some X-rated late-night goodies, there's no place like the **Pink Pussycat Boutique** (tel 305/448–7656, 3094 Fuller St., Coconut Grove). We're talking feathers, condoms, edible underwear, and handcuffs, presented in a sort of salacious supermarket staffed by a little old lady who sits behind the counter. Shop or browse until the store shuts down at 2am. If you need a love glove—and fast—head to **Condomania** (in Coconut Grove, tel 305/445–7729, 3066 Grand Ave; in South Beach, tel 305/531–7872, 760 Washington Ave.) The selection of condoms verges on the whimsical: cherry- or banana-flavored, thin, thick, ribbed, on key chains, on T-shirts. If you're gay or just curious, **GW** (tel 305/534–4763, 720 Lincoln Rd., Miami Beach) stays open until 10pm weekdays and 11pm weekends. The clientele here is mostly gay, but straight men and women stroll in and scope the place out. Besides the dildos and self-help sex books, curious customers may find the Anne Rice vampire chronicles in paperback and comics (many of the Crumb-y underground variety).

Stargazing... We're not talking Madonna or Sly. We're talking about the stars that will shine long after the Material Girl and Rambo are gone. Members of the **Southern Cross Astronomical Society** bring out their high-powered telescopes every Saturday night to view the Miami sky. The celestial happening takes place at the 30-acre Bill Sadowksi Park (17555 SW 79th Ave; Miami), and the club welcomes even those who can't distinguish between the Dippers. Some folks make a picnic out of it. For another look at the stars and planets, head to the **Miami Planetarium** (tel 305/854–2222; 3280 S. Miami Ave., Coconut Grove; multiple nighttime shows on

Fridays and Saturdays with the last one starting at midnight; admission $6). For indoor stars, check out the Planetarium's laser light shows that are accompanied by the music of Nirvana and Pink Floyd (you guessed it—with tracks from *Dark Side of the Moon*).

For caffiends... While Starbucks franchises sweep the rest of the nation, Miami offers something refreshingly different to visitors who like to relax over a cup of coffee. Well, perhaps "relax" isn't the word for what one does over a cafecito, the powerful Cuban brew that comes in small, prescription-strength portions. To sample the real thing, make a pilgrimage to **Versailles** (see the Bar Scene), a Calle Ocho institution where you just might run into Gloria Estefan. Locals and notables alike have been visiting this restaurant for more than twenty years, and chances are none has dozed off accidentally. Of course, larger, less potent brews are also available at the many Miami coffee houses which stay up all night. Nestle amongst the late-night loungers nibbling on dessert with their coffee in the sidewalk cafe at SoBe's **Java Junkies**, or hang out with the college crowd at **Joffrey's** in the Grove, which stays open past midnight (see The Bar Scene).

Nosh 'round the clock... Despite Miami's rep for 24-hour frolics, you'll find more places to buy sex toys than food (well, both satisfy an appetite). The finest edibles around are at **Stephane's Gourmet Market** (tel 305/674–1760; 1430 Washington Ave., Miami Beach; open until midnight and two hours later on weekends), attractively located right in the heart of Washington Avenue and across the street from Liquid and the Cameo. The real item, complete with exotic sandwiches and foodstuffs from Europe, Stephane's outdoes the competition by staying open until the wee hours. An upstairs restaurant is actually quite cozy early in the evening. For those who thought chain drugstores with fast-food counters no longer existed, **Walgreens** (in Miami Beach, tel 305/531–9922, 1845 Alton Rd;. in Miami, tel 305/221–5013, 8850 Coral Way) will come as a revelation; in fact, it's almost retrohip for after-hours munchies. Some Walgreens are open 24 hours daily. For more serious groceries, head to one of several **Hyde Park Markets** (in

Miami Beach, tel 305/531–4972, 700 41st St.; in Surfside, tel 305/861–5301. 9400 Harding Ave.; open nightly until midnight).

Let there be music... You leave a club and that one
song throbs insistently. Where do you go at 1am to buy
the CD? Try **Uncle Sam's Music** (tel 305/532–0973,
1141 Washington Ave., Miami Beach; open until 2am),
where you can get tapes, vinyl, and posters, too. The
store also stocks dance-music collections only heard in
clubs, if you're desperate to play the deejay's mix at your
next "house" party. Inside this between-club hangout
buzz rave-happy club kids rummaging through bins featuring such bands as Nine Inch Nails and Rancid. A few
blocks away is the grand music store, **Spec's** (in South
Beach, tel 305/534–3667, 501 Collins Ave; in Coconut
Grove, tel 305/461–8661, 2982 Grand Ave.). A seemingly endless escalator takes music mavens to music
heaven, where they'll find everything from calypso to
classical, from disco to Disney tunes. There are head-
phones galore for CD sampling (though those alternative types can monopolize them like New Yorkers at pay
phones.) Not to be outdone in the hip department, the
South Beach location features a small coffee shop, in
case you need to put more hop in your hip. A few miles
away is the **CD Solution** (tel 305/662–7100, 1590 S.
Dixie Hwy., Miami; open until midnight), a virtual
shrine to the music gods with wall-to-wall CDs, both
new and used. If you hear that hypnotic tune on the car
radio, just pull over and scour the store for the song.
The store sits in a little plaza, where the mallrats hang
out between flicks.

Drive time... In Miami, you are what you drive. Out on
the street you'll see the young, the posing, and the
vehicularly endowed trolling in their cars. The hottest
runway (yes, just as in fashion model) is **Ocean Drive**
(Miami Beach, from 1st to 15th sts.), thick with teens
and twentysomethings cruising the strip, hooting their
"Hey Mamas" as if on Spring Break in Daytona.
Mondo bazooka speakers thud and pulse from the
hottest Jags to the smallest Geos. When traffic is at its
peak (usually 8pm to midnight), it can take a good hour
or so to go from one end of the street to the other. Just

think of it as living theater without intermission—and without even having to leave your car seat: homeless, been here; drag queens, still here; illegal immigrants, trying to stay here. And then there are the wannabe models strutting up and down and hoping to be, um, discovered. You find the same action on parallel **Washington Avenue.**

Over in the Grove, a similar scene holds up car and pedestrian traffic on the **Main Highway.** The crowd here runs more toward frat boys, Courtney/Kurt disciples, and the Hispanic look-at-me-and-my-car-and-my-babe set. The car radios tend to get louder as they approach **Cocowalk**, home to the Baja Beach Club. It's where the guys drink and hone in on the bikini-clad, Baywatch-like waitresses who literally serve Jell-O drinks from their D-cups. Cruising **Coral Gables Villages** you'll find city founder George Merrick's pockets of international architecture sprinkled throughout. Fortunately, many of the most spectacular architectural examples are either spotlit or illuminated from within (or you can always train a flashlight on the detail work). The most eye-catching and photoworthy is **Chinese Village**, on the 5100 block of Riviera Drive, a compound of about a half-dozen homes painted in vivid hues—including one that's fire-engine red—and embellished with carvings and balconies and visions of Beijing. You can spot **French Normandy Village**, on the 400 block of Viscaya Avenue, by the wooden beams crisscrossing the facades. The houses of **Dutch South African Village**, on Le Jeune Road, have fancy chimneys and vanilla-ice-cream scrollwork. Along the northern border of Coral Gables, Merrick designed eight whizbang entrances to his planned city; only four were completed, all on SW Eighth (known locally as Calle Ocho, the main artery of Little Havana), with columns and pergolas and ornamental urns. Check out the **Douglas Entrance** on SW Eighth Street and Douglas Avenue, a grand gateway bedecked with a tower and twin two-story wings originally intended as work spaces for artists. The **Granada Entrance**, on Granada Boulevard, towers at 60 feet and was built to copy the entryway to Granada, Spain. The most ornate is the **Country Club Prado Entrance**, at the junction of

Eighth and Country Club Prado Boulevard, fashioned like a slice of a formal Italian garden, with pillars, urns, wrought ironwork, fetching vines, and a fountain.

For cruising of another sort... **Sea Kruz** (tel 305/ 538–8300, 1280 5th St., Miami Beach, admission charged) is the quintessential booze cruise in all its vulgar glory, a nautical adventure barely worth the waves it bounces over. The four-hour cruises troll just far enough out to sea to legalize gambling. Beefy guys with tight gold chains who are likely to call women "chicks" hover around the buffet, heaping their plates with seconds and thirds, and the casino is thick with poodle-haired secretaries cranking the arms of the one-arm bandits. Entertainers in the *Saturday Night Fever*-ish lounge probably cut their teeth at some Holiday Inn in Jersey. Don't forget the Dramamine. Seven canary-yellow **Water Taxis** (tel 954/467–6677; operate until 2:30am; fee charged) shuttle around downtown on Biscayne Bay, along the Intracoastal waterways, and down the Miami River. The best time to ride is dusk, when the sunset has thrown its oranges at the sky and the lights of the downtown skyscrapers crank up their kilowatts. Behind Bayside Marketplace, tethered to barber-striped pilings, two gondolas bob amidst a flotilla of party boats for hire. Cheesy though it may seem, a sunset ride à deux on this vessel is a guaranteed jump start to romance. The gondolier stands discreetly astern (with eyes fixed on the bay, not on you, supposedly) and paddles through the quiet waters while nature spray paints the sky. Of the garish gaggle of boats that surround the gondola, **La Rumba** (tel 305/864–6204; Bayside Marketplace; fee charged)—striped with hot pink, aqua, and lime green neon—earns the most points for the kind of campy fun you'd expect from a floating disco. With the throbbing beat of Latin music pulsating from its second-story dance floor, La Rumba does a 90-minute tour of the bay.

Fab fests... March's weeklong **Carnaval Miami**, one of the nation's grandest Latino festivals, gyrates with bacchanalian fervor surpassed perhaps only by Rio's pre-Lenten blowout. Carnaval Night itself kicks off at the

Orange Bowl and culminates in the Calle Ocho Festival, a 23-block street party that deserves an "R" rating for its dirty dancing, tangy food, and hip-twitching music. During the **Coconut Grove Arts Festival**—the city's largest, most popular, and most sprawling art festival, held in mid-February—the bohemian bayside village of Coconut Grove closes its main streets to all but foot traffic, and stall after stall offers art in every imaginable form, from local amateurs to international names. There are often walking tours available in the evenings during the event. **The Miami Film Festival**, a 10-day movie (and party) marathon held in early February, has distinguished itself as the launching pad for films from Latin America and Spain (see The Arts). On the last Sunday of the year, the **King Mango Strut**, the gay and bohemian antidote to the Orange Bowl Parade, draws hundreds of revelers to Coconut Grove. The King Mango crowd includes groups like the Marching Freds (black, white, old, young, fat, skinny—the only thing these guys have in common is that they're all named Fred); they crown their own drag Queen Mango, who reigns over the wacky festivities, which careen and carouse well into the night (see Down and Dirty for more information on all of the above).

The write stuff... It's late and you want something to read. At Mitchell Kaplan's two **Books and Books** branches (in Coral Gables, tel 305/442–4408, 296 Aragon Ave., open nightly until 11pm except Sun until 8pm; in Miami Beach, tel 305/532–3222, 933 Lincoln Rd., open weeknights and Sun until 11pm, Fri and Sat until midnight), bibliophiles can check out the readings, book signings, and reading groups that turn the store into a social gathering spot for literary locals. The Gables store is the mother ship, with more titles, but the meet market is in a built-in cruising ground, the Russian Bear Cafe. At least two nights a week, both bookstores host author readings and book signings that double as socials for the sort of people who religiously read the *New York Times Book Review*. Aspiring writers and poets hoping to be heard and read can be part of **Writers in the Sand** (tel 305/531–6781 ext. 201; Lincoln Center Hotel, 1627 Euclid Ave., Miami Beach; open Wed until 8pm). Talk Shakespeare, debate local columnist Carl

Hiaasen's latest comic diatribes (he's the Herb Caen of Miami), or simply hang with local scribes.

Tattoo you... Tattoos used to be the domain of renegade bikers and nasty pirates. Goody-two shoes didn't go here, but hey, fashion happens. These days Sean Penn, Roseanne, Whoopi Goldberg, Dennis Rodman, and millions of ordinary folks have rolled up their sleeves and pulled down their pants to get inked in the name of trendiness. So, if you think your love will last (or always wanted to be perpetually strangled by a python), try **South Beach Tattoo** (tel 305/538–0104; 861 Washington Ave., South Beach; open until 2am). The walls are papered with designs that range from modest to mega. Another South Beach inkwell is **Tattoos by Lou** (tel 305/532–7300; 231 14th St., Miami Beach; open until 3am). The collection of tattoos is really a *Who's Who* of famous cartoon chums: Tweety Bird, Sylvester the Cat, Bugs, Spiderman, and the Man of Steel.

Flowers... Your girlfriend's in a huff because you objected to her dancing with that CK-model lookalike wearing little more than his boxers. But how to make amends at 1am? Stroll into **Cocowalk** (3015 Grand Ave., Coconut Grove) and flag down one of the "floating" flower vendors selling roses and carnations. You can catch these roving florists in the plaza, day in, night out, until well past midnight. You can also usually find them up **Main Highway**, off the mall. In Miami Beach, they work **Washington Avenue**. The prices vary and are often negotiable, especially around 3am. The really desperate have been seen rummaging through the garbage of **Berens Flowers** (tel 305/673–5853; 1502 Washington Ave., Miami Beach), where scavengers have found sunflowers and other bruised but aromatic rewards.

When the art bug bites... At Miami Beach's **Lincoln Road Gallery Walk,** a string of galleries on the Lincoln Road Mall opens their doors until about 11pm on the first weekend of every month. Most of the galleries offer the requisite wine and munchies to accompany the displays of predominantly pan-American, 20th-century art. Lincoln Road's Gallery Walk features, among other things, the classic looks of Barbara Gillman, whose establishment was one of the first to take the Miami art scene serious-ly. Portraits of jazz artists may hang alongside classic Floridian postcards done to a fare-thee-well, but you'll always find something curious. Farther east, the pop Valhalla of Romero Britto continues to roll along, foist-ing his cartoon-like, bubble-gum-colored images on all the world (perhaps you've seen his Absolut creation). As part of the **Coral Gables Gallery Walk** (tel 305/444–4493; first Fri of every month, open 7–10pm), a curious trolley takes the faithful to such "genius galleries" as the Fred Snitzer, which showcases the work of Cuban mas-ters such as Wilfredo Lam. Most of the twenty-odd Gables galleries show heartrending Latin art (and dreck, too), which yet again sets the Miami scene apart from any other in the country.

    The Holocaust Memorial (tel 305/538–1663; Dade Blvd. and Meridian Ave., Miami Beach; open until 9pm) sees more than 600 visitors a day, who come to view the 42-foot bronze giant hand that reaches up to the sky. Below it are depictions of human horrors, lifelike mannequins of people with suffering etched across their faces. The World War II Holocaust memo-rial includes 50 eerie photographs as well as lists of concentration-camp victims. Many of the exhibits of the **Historical Museum of South Florida** (tel 305/375–1492; 101 W. Flagler St., Miami; open Thurs until 9pm; admission charged) focus on the Tequesta and Seminole Indians, who lived here long before South Beach became SoBe. Ceramics, artifacts, clothing, tools, as well as other historical goodies like 18th-century cannons and art-deco streetcars fill the display cases; the place usually swarms with grade-schoolers on field trips during the day, but Thursday night draws a more sophisticated crowd. (You half expect to see Peter Matthiessen researching his next novel.) In the same compound, the exhibition space at downtown Miami's **Center for the Fine Arts** (tel 305/375–3000; 101 W. Flagler St., Miami; open Thur until 9pm; admission charged) always sports a new look. With no permanent collection, the museum instead selects from the most topical and provocative of the current shows traveling the art world. It's refreshingly unstuffy, worth a trip on a rainy Thursday night—and a premier place to collect the Eurotrash.

Street musicians... Hey, Tracy Chapman got started in
Boston this way, serenading waiting subway passengers.
The outdoor fountain at **World Resources** restaurant (tel
305/534–9095; 719 Lincoln Rd., Miami Beach), always
swirling with incense, is the site of some of the funkiest
alfresco live music in town. It might be folkie protest
music or a sitar concert; performances kick off weekends
at 8pm. Maybe you'll get lucky and your visit will coin-
cide with a full-moon drum happening. For music by the
bay, dock yourself at **Bayside Marketplace** (tel 305/577–
3344; 401 Biscayne Blvd., Miami), Miami's answer to
Boston's Faneuil Hall, where you'll find everything from
a Hard Rock Cafe to the Disney Store, and tourists
milling about with Goofy looks (well, the cruise ships
pull right up to the dock). During the afternoons and
evenings, local talent sings and sways to salsa sounds, Top
40, and some reggae. Just about anything goes in this
smorgasbord of bands that changes daily. Another local
attraction—although we don't know whether to call them
musicians—are the **Hare Krishnas,** whose chanting and
tambourine tapping often draws catcalls from the
punked-out crowd. See them do their thing at the
Grove's **Cocowalk** (3015 Grand Ave.). As the shades of
evening roll in, you'll find these guys in front of the
plaza, jumping and humming and circling around.

Storytelling... Hear the stories that haunt the famous
Biltmore Hotel (tel 305/445–1926, ask the concierge for
storytelling information; 1200 Anastasia Ave., Coral
Gables; Thur 7pm at the fireside in the lobby), a
Mediterranean-style confection jutting into the Coral
Gables night sky. Storyteller Linda Spitzer spins legends
of this historic, Disneyesque castle—unoccupied for a
time until a mid-1980s renovation, before which pigeons
and bats were apparently the most frequent drop-ins—
that boasts a towering Spanish-style spire, one of the
biggest hotel pools in the country, marble for miles, and
plush carpets. A preview: Fats Walsh, bodyguard to a
New York mobster, was rubbed out here in 1929 and,
supposedly, his shade resides in the Everglades Suite on
the 13th floor.

Nighttime shopping... Malls tend to run until at least 9
at night. Businesses in South Beach and Coconut Grove

MIAMI ⟨ HANGING OUT

usually stay open later than their downtown or Gables counterparts, often until 11 or midnight. Mallrats will be in hog heaven in Miami. For the most part, of course, malls are to shopping as McDonald's is to dining: familiar, convenient, and palatable, sure, but they offer few surprises, few insights, and precious little that's different from one city to another. Most of the dozen or so biggies in Miami are pretty much interchangeable, distinguishable only by nuance or the style of their architecture. Here's a quick rundown: Though it ably satisfies fundamental retail-therapy needs, the **Dadeland Mall** (tel 305/661–7582; U.S. 1 and Kendall Dr.), in Kendall, Miami's über-suburb to the south, is mind-numbingly large and generic. Farther south, the **Falls** (tel 305/255–4570; U.S. 1 and SW 136th St.), a planned community of shopping centers, is a bit lovelier and snootier: Bloomingdale's and pricier specialty shops zigzag around waterfalls, wooden boardwalks, and robust foliage. The **Aventura Mall** (tel 305/935–1110; 19501 Biscayne Blvd.), in the 'burbs near the northern county line, is anchored by the ever-reliable Lord & Taylor and Macy's; the usual Gap-type chains take up the rest of the space. The **Miracle Center** (tel 305/444-8890; 301 Coral Way), a credit-card toss away from Coral Gables, is one of the least exciting buildings designed by Arquitectonica, the local firm responsible for the whimsical glass boxes on Brickell Avenue (seen in the opening montage of "Miami Vice"). The interior—160 standard-mall stores—is unfortunately as uneventful as the exterior. The setting and the vistas at the 16-acre waterfront **Bayside Marketplace** (tel 305/577–3344; 401 Biscayne Blvd.), on the other hand, do make it worth stopping; the standard-issue mall stores and artsy-craftsy specialty shops here service herds of cruise-ship passengers from the nearby port.

Mayfair Shops (tel 305/448–1700; 2911 Grand Ave.) and **CocoWalk** (tel 305/444–0777; 3015 Grand Ave.) face each other on two prime corners of Coconut Grove. With its fountains, sculpted metal ornamentation, and self-conscious designer concept, Mayfair fairly screams "upscale!" Its smallish shops display goods with large price tags (mostly Waspy designers like Jil Sander, Ralph Lauren, and the nouveau classic Ann Taylor).

CocoWalk is a trilevel, open-air Mediterranean-style shopping center. On the weekends, (when its 550-car garage is filled by 7pm), all of Miami's pre-washed, jeans-clad youth and whatnot seem to converge here. Coco-Walk is home to 39 mall tenants, including the Gap, Banana Republic, Blockbuster Music, B. Dalton Bookstore, and an AMC 16-screen cineplex. The architecture and atmosphere are a cross between the funky and fashionable, with a mix of open areas, balconies, and balustrades. The salmon-colored plaza bustles from noon well into the wee hours. This place has an artsy festival feeling, with strolling mimes and jugglers, musicians and artisans, roving florists, packed bars, dance clubs, and retail shops. The complex gets more than 3 million visitors a year. The B. Dalton bookstore stays open until 1am. Cafe Tu Tu Tango features performance artists in the middle of a dining room, where colorful appetizers and tapas (and people) are the main course, and the Cheescake Factory has taken to giving patrons beepers so they can stroll the Grove while they wait to be called to their tables. And the line outside Baja Beach Club, a bustling dance spot on the upper level, doesn't begin to fade until well past 2am. If the coterie of collegians, yuppies, couples, young and old, are not eating or dancing, they are shopping. The Gap and its army of euphoric Gap clerks work until midnight, in case one has to buy a last-minute cardigan for the night. Victoria's Secret lets women and their men browse bras and silk teddies till the witching hour. The bored and curious tend to stroll into Roscoe & Bernie's Cards and Gifts to tinker and play with odd toys like life-size Captain Kirk stand-up posters and furry toy kittens that meow and purr like the real thing.

The consortium of chic in north Miami Beach is the collection of designer-fashion boutiques known as **Bal Harbour Shops** (tel 305/866–0311; 9700 Collins Ave.; open until 9pm Mon, Thur, Fri). Only 24-carat names pay rent here: Cartier, Saks Fifth Avenue, Gucci, Hermès, Charles Jourdan. You get the picture. If the idea of paying $400 for a pair of shoes makes you a little queasy, though, beat a quick retreat to **Sawgrass Mills** (tel 954/846–2353; 12801 W. Sunrise Blvd., Sunrise; open till 9:30pm Mon–Sat, till 8 Sun), which is hyped as the world's largest outlet mall.

More than 200 stores—Ann Taylor, Nine West, and scads of others—are laid out in a mile-long alligator-shaped mega-mall west of Fort Lauderdale. Regulars swear the bargains are worth the 40-minute drive.

Predictably, SoBe offers the most eclectic assortment of goodies. Owner Gloria Anderson's **Last Tango in Paradise** (tel 305/532–4228; 1214 Washington Ave.) resembles the closet of some aging glamorous movie star (without the skeletons—or wire hangers). For sale are beaded gowns, feather boas, vintage tuxedos, and racks full of well-maintained vintage clothing. The customers range from matrons on a nostalgia trip to drag queens looking for the scene-stealing chiffon. The arts and crafts of the Third World crowd the racks and shelves at **Island Trading Company** (tel 305/673–6300; 1332 Ocean Dr.). The selection includes straw hats from Zaire, pillows from Zimbabwe, wooden bowls from South Africa, and all the fabrics, clothing, and accoutrements you need to signal your retail participation in the global community. The windows at **Lunatika** (tel 305/534–8585; 1671 Michigan Ave.) glow on through the night with the iridescence created by its stock of whimsical, if not downright outrageous, lamps.

If the body is the ultimate beach accessory, then the bathing suit is your subculture ID card. On *las playas de la ciudad* (the beaches of the city) anything goes, and usually does—tangas (thongs), G-strings, slimming black one-piecers, smaller-than-Speedos for the buffed boyz, retro numbers for the style council, baggies, boxers, and those preppie Tommy Hilfiger numbers. And needless to say, your cover-ups will be just as highly scrutinized. Miami masters of the artfully casual gravitate toward shorts, tank tops, skirts, sandals, loose clothing, and natural fibers. **Ete** (tel 305/672–4742; 714 Lincoln Rd.) may have a bit too many trendoid fashions that will undoubtedly show up before year's end as Glamour "don'ts," but they also stock all sorts of swimsuits, classically cut sundresses, trousers, and blouses with just the right amount of slouch to be comfortable and the right amount of cachet to be (quietly) stylish. Though the fashion police would probably arrest anyone who took the Armani name in vain, the designer's lower-end boutique, **A/X, Armani Exchange** (tel 305/531–5900; 760 Collins Ave.), seems all huff, puff, and bluff. Jeans and cotton shirts are the staples (ho hum), along with a healthy dose of attitude from a staff afflicted by the cheap ennui of beautiful youth. Finally, SoBe doesn't hold a monopoly on casual chic resort wear or housewares. In the Grove, **Salo Design** (tel 305/443–1861; 3141 Commodore Plaza) sells jewelry (from traditional to cutting edge), vases, wall hangings, wind chimes, and small decorative objects crafted by artists and artisans from all 50 states. Owner Yvonne Grassie (whose work is also on display) prices her goods to sell, not to stun.

late nigh

t dining

The Miami restaurant
scene, especially after dark,
is pure living theater
(sometimes of the absurd).
While the chefs strive to
please both the eye and
palate, painting their dishes

like a fauve canvas in bright bold colors, the style police also excel at presentation. It's a fashion parade, from polyester to punk, as designed by Fellini. Just like the streets themselves, it's a fun—if hardly free—taste of all Miami has to offer. The decor (ranging from pre-Castro Cuban opulence bordering on bordellos to uncomfortable Minimalist furnishings mellowed by art-deco seashell tones), ambience (from Ricky Ricardo's Club Tropicana to retro beatnik hip), waitstaff (all CK One rejects striking an attitude) and clientele (Eurotrash and their American apostles, with a few lobster-hued tourists in loud Hawaiian shirts thrown in for color) are often as entertaining and eclectic as the cuisine itself.

Which is not to say that the food is merely incidental. The Miamian melting pot guarantees diners a savvy, savory gastronomic stew. Some of the terms used by chefs like Mark Militello (Mark's Place), Allen Susser (Chef Allen's), Michael Schwartz (Nemo) and Guillermo Veloso (Yuca) to describe their fare are a mouthful in and of themselves. New Floridian, New World, Pan-Atlantic, Tropical Floribbean, Equatorial, Asian/Southwestern/Caribbean Fusion, Light American Spa cuisines, anyone? Even Little Havana's Calle Ocho has entered the nineties with culinary abandon, instituting la nueva cocina Cubana.

Not that the Institutions have retreated—you can still grapple with a Joe's Stone Crab; dig into delish deli with the cane set at Wolfie's (where gum-cracking Jewish-Mom waitresses will even offer the occasional drag queen advice on her nail polish); or scarf down classic pub grub at Tobacco Road while listening to hot blues brothers (and sisters). But this pan-American outpost spiced by a grab-bag of cultures now offers a virtual U.N. of gustatory experiences. In addition to the expected cosmopolitan choices (French, Chinese, Mexican, Indian, Japanese, Italian), seemingly every country in the Caribbean basin and South America is represented: from Jamaica (jerk pork so spicy it would make a Texan's eyes water) to Argentinian (with parrilladas—grills—featuring every calorie- and cholesterol-laden meat under the fierce Miamian sun). The most fun, of course, is when chefs mix and match cultures with fine contempt for more orthodox couplings: rock-shrimp hash with mango ketchup, green plantain linguini, or ribs in guava sauce. They cull their hybrid inspirations from Miami's bountiful marketplace: not just oranges and grapefruits here—oh no, we have carambola and mamey. And why flounder in flounder or grope for grouper when alligator is yours for the asking?

How To Dress

First, dearies, you have to fit in to get in. So to wit, a few fashion tips. South Florida's weather has permanently tipped the dress code toward casual. Even in the winter months, the weather rarely becomes cold enough for cashmere, so leave that fur behind in the deep freeze. Whatever the season, think function first, fashion second. For example, chuck the pantyhose (yes, even with the clever sparkle—unless of course you're doing drag): Miami can be oppressively hot and humid. Stick with loose, comfortable cotton and linen. Many locals consider dressing down to be dressing up, especially in flavor-of-the-moment South Beach. On the other hand, tonier spots in Coral Gables and Coconut Grove beg for a bead or two, ladies. And men, remember the no-tie, boxy linen jacket, Euro-trouser look introduced by "Miami Vice" in the eighties? It still goes, appropriate for a sidewalk meal in South Beach and the Gables alike. (But Don Johnson stubble is out, greasy pony tail/mangy scruff à la Brad Pitt is in.) Latinos tend to ornament themselves more than your average vacationing gringo; if you're heading for a Little Havana hot spot, you might want to gussy it up a bit. In general, leave the Miami Beach T-shirts at your hotel and try to dress as au courant as possible to help the restaurant raise its property values.

When To Eat

Unless you want to save a few bucks and watch the geriatric set (or as club kids call them, "the I.V. drips"), avoid the early-bird specials. In fact, don't even sniff around for a table until 9pm; some South Beach eateries don't heat up until 11pm. Speaking of which, in Miami it's not what you eat, it's where you eat. In South Beach, Calle Ocho, and the Gables, dining out isn't a refueling pitstop but rather a chance to peacock. The hottest spots (like Nemo, China Grill, and Hotel Astor all in South Beach) require reservations up to a week in advance; for most others, early in the day will do. To snag last-minute tables, call between 7 and 8pm the night you want to dine—that's the witching hour when cancellations are called in. Your hotel concierge might exert some pull (with a little push). Or go straight to the source if you want to avoid being seated in Siberia. All maitre d's and hostesses here speak the international language of assistance: cash. There are more greased palms than coconut palms in South Beach.

There: you've navigated Miami's dining out protocol and etiquette. Now sit back and enjoy the show—unless, of course, you intend to audition yourselves.

Miami Area Late Night Dining

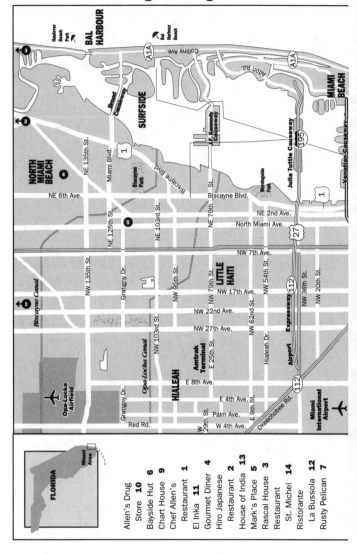

Allen's Drug
  Store **10**
Bayside Hut **6**
Chart House **9**
Chef Allen's
  Restaurant **1**
El Inka **11**
Gourmet Diner **4**
Hiro Japanese
  Restaurant **2**
House of India **13**
Mark's Place **5**
Rascal House
  Restaurant **3**
St. Michel
  Ristorante **14**
La Bussola **12**
Rusty Pelican **7**

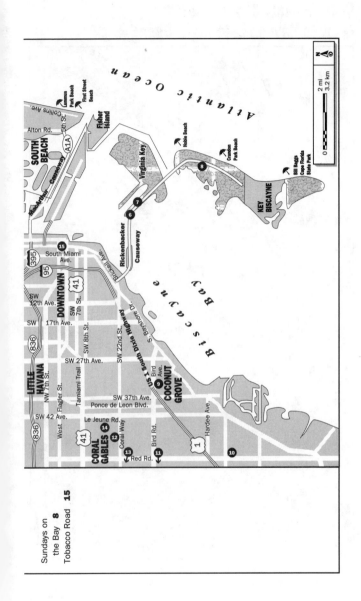

Atlantic Ocean

Lummus
Park Beach
First Street
Beach

Fisher
Island

Alton Rd.

5th St.

Collins Ave.

SOUTH
BEACH

A1A

MacArthur Causeway

Virginia Key

Hobie Beach

Crandon
Park Beach

8

Bill Baggs
Cape Florida
State Park

KEY
BISCAYNE

7

6

Rickenbacker Causeway

Brickell Ave.

395

95

15

South Miami
Ave.

41

DOWNTOWN

SW
12th Ave.

SW
7th St.

SW
17th Ave.

836

SW 8th St.

LITTLE
HAVANA

NW 7th St.

SW 27th Ave.

Tamiami Trail

West Flagler St.

41

SW 22nd St.

SW 37th Ave.

Ponce de Leon Blvd.

Le Jeune Rd.

14

Coral Way

CORAL
GABLES

12

13

Red Rd.

US 1 South Dixie Highway

S. Bayshore Dr.

Bird
Ave.

COCONUT
GROVE

9

Bird Rd.

11

1

Hardee Ave.

10

Biscayne Bay

2 mi
3.2 km
0

N

Sundays on
the Bay   8
Tobacco Road 15

Coral Gables, Coconut Grove & Little Havana Late Night Dining

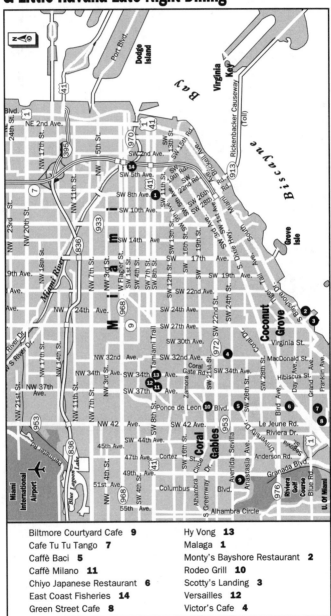

Biltmore Courtyard Cafe **9**		Hy Vong **13**
Cafe Tu Tu Tango **7**		Malaga **1**
Caffè Baci **5**		Monty's Bayshore Restaurant **2**
Caffè Milano **11**		Rodeo Grill **10**
Chiyo Japanese Restaurant **6**		Scotty's Landing **3**
East Coast Fisheries **14**		Versailles **12**
Green Street Cafe **8**		Victor's Cafe **4**

Miami Beach Late Night Dining

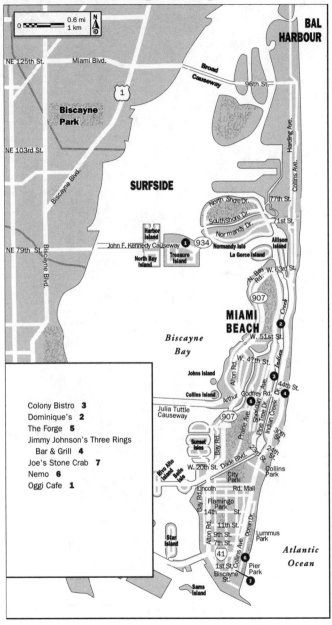

Colony Bistro **3**
Dominique's **2**
The Forge **5**
Jimmy Johnson's Three Rings
  Bar & Grill **4**
Joe's Stone Crab **7**
Nemo **6**
Oggi Cafe **1**

South Beach Late Night Dining

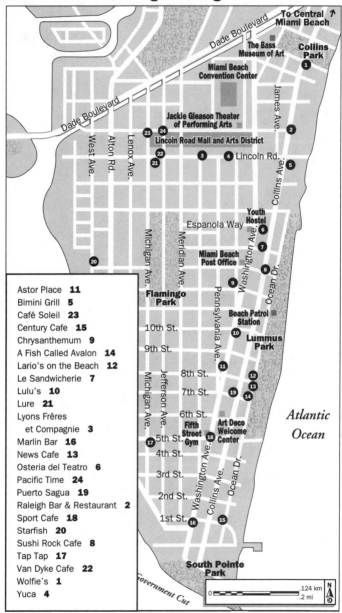

Astor Place **11**
Bimini Grill **5**
Café Soleil **23**
Century Cafe **15**
Chrysanthemum **9**
A Fish Called Avalon **14**
Lario's on the Beach **12**
Le Sandwicherie **7**
Lulu's **10**
Lure **21**
Lyons Frères
  et Compagnie **3**
Marlin Bar **16**
News Cafe **13**
Osteria del Teatro **6**
Pacific Time **24**
Puerto Sagua **19**
Raleigh Bar & Restaurant **2**
Sport Cafe **18**
Starfish **20**
Sushi Rock Cafe **8**
Tap Tap **17**
Van Dyke Cafe **22**
Wolfie's **1**
Yuca **4**

The Lowdown

See-and-be-scenes... South Beach's Ocean Drive is shoulder to shoulder with outdoor cafes spilling from cotton candy–colored art-deco hotels. **Caffè Milano** is one of the best if you're in the mood for noise, fashion, attitude, and new-wave Italian cooking. This proudly hip restaurant is a favorite of models, groovesters, and Eurotrash who petulantly pick at their osso buco and pasta dishes, scanning the room for others more beautiful, more famous. The Augustus salad with hearts of palm and crab is something everyone should experience at least once in a lifetime. At the southern tip of South Beach sits **Nemo**, an intimate restaurant with urban-contempo decor, a young, arty crowd, and an organic, New American menu. It's one of South Beach's hottest spots, and it can be hard to get a reservation for dinner, especially on weekends. Once you've snagged that prize table, try curried lentil stew, wok-charred salmon, or phyllo-wrapped prawns with salsa. Part of the stylish scene, but not as screamingly trendy, the **Raleigh Restaurant & Bar** in the exquisitely renovated 1940s oceanfront Raleigh Hotel is under the culinary supervision of chef Marc Lippman, whose New American menu includes spa cuisine disguised as tasty, filling meals. Recent selections included lamb sausage and couscous seasoned with mint, and roasted grouper with a veggie sauce. After dinner, stroll outside, dip your toes in the palm-encircled pool and dream of Esther Williams. **Pacific Time** on South Beach's Lincoln Road Mall sports an East-meets-West menu and feeds a crowd that favors asymmetrical haircuts and a Gap-inspired wardrobe. Chef and co-owner Jonathan Eismann's menu changes regularly, but includes such Pacific Rim innovations as tempura-fried sweet potatoes; grouper with sake, shallots, and ginger; and catfish stuffed with ginger. For the best people viewing, dine after 10pm or park at the bar and sip a Campari and soda, watching the street scene parade by on the mall. At the **Blue Door** restaurant in the hyperstylish Delano Hotel in Miami Beach, the patrons are as visually tasty as the food. This is South Beach's latest *in* spot (Madonna is part owner), and here at glamour ground zero it is considered très gauche to dine before 10. During winter months reservations can be hard to come by (sometimes you need to phone two to three weeks in advance), but if you do secure a coveted table, observe some unwritten ground rules: Don't gawk if, say, Robin Williams or John Travolta is dining at the table beside yours. Dress to the nines, or better yet, the tens. Don't blanch at the check. And order anything from the imaginative menu: tuna tartare with quail egg, baked crab cakes with fennel salad, or the roast duck in sour-cherry sauce. The chef at **Astor Place** in South Beach's Astor Hotel favors New American barbecue; most entrées are smoked or grilled, like the wild-mushroom pancakes, jerk tuna, or cowboy-grilled prime rib. But who's looking at the food? In this stunningly restored vintage art-deco hotel, the clientele is more distracting than the architecture. Herds of beautiful people flock here to one of SoBe's restaurant newcomers. And the South Beach dinner law is in place here: The later the hour, the better-looking the crowd.

Institutions... At the top of the you-must-eat-here-or-else-you-won't-have-sampled-the-*real*-Miami restaurant list is **Joe's Stone Crab**. This landmark at the southern tip of South Beach has been around since 1913, and its reputation hasn't flagged. No reservations are accepted, and lines often snake around the block. Inside the cavernous dining room—the tile floors amplify the din—patrons don plastic bibs and dig into the tried-and-true combo: black-tipped stone-crab claws (jumbo are best) stuffed with tender meat and accompanied by creamed spinach, a crispy nest of hash browns, and a tangy wedge of Key lime pie for dessert. For those bent on immediate gratification, **Joe's Take Away**, adjacent to the main restaurant, sells stone crabs and side orders to go. For a big feed before a fat night of dancing or clubbing try the **Rascal House** deli and restaurant in North Miami Beach, where they've been serving latkes, knishes, and brisket since the 1950s, from menus as long as a Michener novel. Career waitresses cluck around the booths and tables that pack in almost 500 patrons. Portions are on the large side, and regulars swear by the corned beef and the chicken soup with kreplach. In a city where restaurants open and close faster than a hibiscus blossom, **Chef Allen's** has, since its opening in 1986, quietly built its reputation as one of Miami's premier venues. The chef in question, Allen Susser (formerly of Le Cirque and a James Beard–award winner), combines Caribbean and Floridian staples to produce knock-out dishes like green papaya slaw, jerk calamari, and swordfish with citrus couscous. The dessert soufflés are legendary (try Dutch cocoa). The stylish patrons sitting in the rosy glow of neon don't seem to mind that the "Miami Vice"-ish decor is a little dated, or that the restaurant is set in the strip-mall stretches of northern Dade County; it's the artwork on the plates that keeps 'em coming back.

For after-midnight munchies... About a half dozen stools sit outside **Le Sandwicherie**, a fast-food spot frequented by the body-pierced, the tattooed, and the nighttime flotsam and jetsam of South Beach. The hip never sleep, or so it seems, at **News Cafe**, ground zero for South Beach's oceanside cafe scene. Inside there are tables and a small international newsstand (thus the name). But outside is where the action is: The tables that crowd the sidewalk are packed through the night with those who come to schmooze, to peruse European magazines, to gaze longingly across the street at the Atlantic Ocean, to ogle the parade of legs-up-to-there models, or, surprisingly, even to eat. The News is a prime spot for light midnight munchies like bagels, pâtés, salads, and fruit plates. At **Wolfie's**, a South Beach fixture since 1947, the world-weary waitresses wear pink polyester dresses and embossed name tags. They also have a tendency to offer advice on anything from your wardrobe ("I'm sorry, dahling, but red is just not your color") to your menu choices ("You need some blintzes. Trust me on this one"). With decor caught in a sixties time warp and a clientele that is heavily geriatric, this Beach institution looks like a diner that time forgot. The food is New York traditional (read: Jewish deli) with vats of pickles, baskets of fresh rolls, and danishes accompanying every order. If that's all a little too heavy for you, consider **Hiro Japanese Restaurant** instead; with a 3:30am closing time, this North Miami spot is perfect for those late-night sushi seizures.

Decor to die for... At **Tap Tap**, a Haitian restaurant on South Beach, almost every surface is emblazoned with high-voltage Caribbean colors, including the vibrant scenes of Haitian life painted on the walls. The crowd here looks as if it stepped out of a Benetton ad. They sip Red Stripe beer at the bar or in one of the half-dozen dining rooms and feast on moderately priced Caribbean meals like lambi (conch), goat, and, once again, jerk chicken. The menu, with its inventive salads and slant toward seafood, is secondary at the **Biltmore Courtyard Cafe** in the historic Biltmore Hotel in Coral Gables. The Spanish Mediterranean architecture is a real feast for the eyes: Built in the 1920s as a replica of the Giralda Tower in Seville, the 26-story hotel looms regally over Coral Gables, with vaulted frescoes, soaring ceilings, and opulent chandeliers lending snob appeal to the public spaces. To best savor the setting, opt for a casual dinner alfresco on Tuesday nights, when diners are serenaded by an opera singer.

Local color... For a ladleful of the pan-American bouillabaisse that is Miami, try **Versailles** on Calle Ocho—you'll get a good introduction to Cuban food and to the range of Anglos and Latinos who live around here. Well-coifed Cubanos, men in guayaberas (short-sleeved cotton shirts), families from the 'burbs, sunburned tourists, and the young and restless pack the brightly lit rooms until the wee hours, sipping café con leche and selecting moderately priced, King Kong–sized portions of Cuban dishes from the laminated menus. If you're a real gringo, play it safe with one of the standbys like *arroz con pollo* (chicken with rice), *ropa vieja* (which means "old clothes" but is actually shredded roast beef in tomato sauce), or *palomillo* (skirt steak). The sidewalk tables at the **News Cafe** on the corner of Eighth Street and Ocean Drive in South Beach provide a ringside view of the nightly Mardi Gras in front of some of the *très* coolest oceanfront real estate in the country. Models, surfer dudes, leather-skinned geriatrics, bladers, bodybuilders, and Eurotourists provide visual hors d'oeuvres; gazers who also want to graze can order salads, sandwiches, and soups both domestic and continental from a U.N. bistro menu. The News buzzes 24 hours a day—indoor tables share space with an international newsstand and bookstore. At the **Van Dyke Cafe** on South Beach, it's the location, people watching, and noisy brasserie feel that draw patrons to this two-story, gazing-and-grazing restaurant in the middle of the Lincoln Road Mall. Tables spill onto the sidewalk, a red British call box stands sentinel, and perma-tanned trendoids blade by. Food is almost an afterthought here, with a standard cafe menu of sandwiches, salads, and pasta dishes.

Consistently the best... Muted pastels set the tone at the North Miami bistro **Mark's Place**—conversations are hushed, corners are softened with plants, and the booth seating encourages earnest tête-à-têtes. There's a refreshing lack of outlandishness at Mark's, perhaps because the emphasis is on the show put on in its open kitchen. A darling of the food press, chef and owner Mark Militello fashions his menu with seasonal fruits and vegetables. Past greatest hits have included fried quail with black-eyed peas and collard greens; jerk pork with red beans, corn, and plantains; and Florida rabbit with polenta. In spite of the surfeit of Italian restaurants arm-wrestling for the attention of South Beach diners, the 12-table **Osteria del Teatro** has earned consistently high marks from local cognoscenti, both for its food and its sexy, noir atmosphere. The blue neon sign out front casts a smoky glow on the faces of the patrons and the unctuous waiters serving tantalizing entrées like salmon and fennel in orange juice. It's often booked weeks in advance, but you never know.

Where you'll be the only tourist... Tucked into an innocuous strip shopping center on the 79th Street Causeway, which ribbons between Miami Beach and the mainland, **Oggi Cafe** has a loyal following of locals who dress down and duck in for fresh, homemade pasta dishes at reasonable prices and courteous service sans attitude. Its reputation must be spreading, though, because the dining room was expanded in 1995; it now holds a couple of dozen tables and an agonizingly tempting display case of desserts. Reservations aren't accepted, but if you elect to wait outside on a bench, the owners bring out a glass of complimentary red wine.

MIAMI ☽ LATE NIGHT DINING

Thirty-six seats squeeze into the tiny Calle Ocho Vietnamese restaurant **Hy Vong**; it must be starting to catch on, though, because locals have reportedly been waiting up to an hour for a table. Many insider foodies consider this Miami's finest—and untrendiest—traditional Asian eatery. House specialties are chicken with lemongrass and dolphin fish with mango and green peppercorns. This is not nouvelle territory: Both the entrées and the desserts are large and filling.

The **Gourmet Diner** in North Miami on Biscayne Boulevard looks deceiving: You'd expect traditional diner fare from this transplanted chrome-and-Formica place, but the food here has a decidedly French twist. Ask for steamed artichokes with tangy pink vinaigrette, escargot aswim in garlic butter, or herb-encrusted lamb. The calorie-unconscious can eenie-meenie-minee-moe their way through an ever-changing list of homemade desserts.

First class with a dress code... It's the exotica that people remember most about the menu at **Dominique's** in the Alexander All-Suite Luxury Hotel in central Miami Beach. You mean you've never tried sautéed buffalo sausage or alligator tail or diamondback rattlesnake salad? Besides the headline-grabbing handful of unorthodox Florida-centric foods, though, Dominique's menu emphasizes traditional French cuisine, and overall, it's a very conservative, grown-up sort of place. Men are required to wear jackets, tuxedoed waiters usher you about, and candlelit tables overlook lush gardens striped with waterfalls. The valet parking stand at **The Forge** in mid–Miami Beach is crowded with Cadillacs, and inside, middle-aged, moneyed men with thinning hair light up cigars at the conclusion of protein-laden, multicourse meals. The dining room would have made Liberace feel right at home: frilly chandeliers, large objets d'art, gilt frames, Tiffany glass, and lots of polished stone surfaces. The Forge's menu tries to be all things to all people (except, perhaps, vegetarians), offering a full range of fish, veal, steaks, and poultry, much of it cooked on an oak grill. Regulars rave about the beef selections and the roasted duck with black currants. The pasta appetizers alone would make a whole meal for some, and the wine list, at a gluttonous 208 pages, is reputed to be the city's fattest.

Nouvelle done well... No stranger to food writers and the popular press, **Yuca**—in Coral Gables and on South Beach's Lincoln Road Mall—has updated many Cuban standbys to produce Nuevo Cubano cuisine. You'll probably need your waiter to translate as you try to decide between green plantain linguine with *sofrito* or *palomillo* veal with *moros*. This is upscale Cuban food for an upscale crowd, where dining lasts until way past midnight.

Quietly stylish and unrelentingly hip, **Pacific Time** on South Beach's Lincoln Road Mall is the place for East-West fusion food. Tasty eclectic entrées like Peking pancakes or tuna over miso noodles with green onions are served in ample portions (which is in itself a departure from the nouvelle creed). What's more, all your needs are cared for in a professionally efficient manner by a good-looking staff who all look as if they're waiting to break into the big time. The **Colony Bistro** is boisterous, glamorous, and in the center of the flash and fanfare of South Beach's Ocean Drive. All of that notwithstanding, it consistently manages to serve innovative food and feature a wait staff that defies sulky South Beach convention with its borderline perkiness. The menu is regularly revised to combine unlikely ingredients with surprising results; a recent dish teamed grilled pompano with seaweed salad, curry-coconut mushrooms, and sticky rice.

Oceanside dining... For prime people watching and alfresco dining accompanied by the cottony white noise of the ocean, aim for an outdoor table at **A Fish Called Avalon** in the Avalon Hotel on South Beach's Ocean Drive. Outside seats may be hard to score in this artfully subdued restaurant; it's built a solid reputation for first-rate SoBe tropical cuisine—fish dishes gussied up with fresh local fruits and veggies—and it has a loyal following of hip and sophisticated regulars (at least they think of themselves as hip and sophisticated). Across the street, palm trees sway and white sands stretch down to the ocean's edge. Former University of Miami football coach and local sports icon Jimmy Johnson has lent his name and a truckload of sports paraphernalia to **Jimmy Johnson's Three Rings Bar & Grill** in the Eden Roc Hotel on the ocean side of Miami Beach. There's a locker-room thing working here, with big-screen TVs programmed to the sports stations and crowds of big-necked men chowing down on burgers and steaks the size of toy poodles. There's a slightly less testosterone-laden, mellower Key West sort of feel to the patio that overlooks the ocean; check out the funky Plexiglas panels on the side of the swimming pool.

Bayside dining... Gargantuan freighters almost dwarf the skyline as they're silently tugged up the Miami River, a working industrial artery that slices though downtown. One of the oldest restaurants on the river (dating from the 1930s), the casual, boisterous **East Coast Fisheries** is housed in a former shrimp packing plant. A fleet of three dozen boats trolls the nearby waters for fresh catches that you'll see displayed on ice inside—grouper, snapper, mackerel, flounder, lobster. The conch-fritter appetizer is almost obligatory.

Bring your camera to dinner at Key Biscayne's **Rusty Pelican**, part of a fishnet-draped national chain: It's the hands-down winner of Miami's undeclared Best-Restaurant-for-a-Sunset competition. There's usually a lively crowd beneath the paddle fans that circle above the bar. A surf-and-turf menu does the job, but the location—surrounded by water on three sides—makes it special; locals know it as the place to bring out-of-town friends to show off the "Miami Vice" skyline. Bayside seats go first, but there are enough views of Biscayne Bay, Key Biscayne, and downtown to go around. Tucked behind a boatyard in Coconut Grove, the **Chart House** sits on Dinner Key Marina at the western edge of Biscayne Bay. At night, diners are hypnotized by the city lights shimmering on the bay and illuminating a thicket of sailboat masts. Beef is what the chef does best, especially the filet mignon and prime rib. Swordfish served in thick slabs and dolphin fish are local seafooders' favorites. Nearby **Scotty's Landing**, tucked beside the Dinner Key Marina, is more like a large backyard party. It's a prime spot for a mellow dinner after a day at the beach. Boaties, marina rats, and perma-tanned old salts park around the bar, munching on fish sandwiches and fries while they size up the sailboats moored at the marina. Umbrellas hover over a couple of dozen outdoor tables at the water's edge; the sound track is the clang of line against mast. Unknown even to many locals, and often confused with the Bayside shopping center, **Bayside Hut** is a waterfront tiki-hut kind of place on Key Biscayne in the shadow of the Miami Marine Stadium. Hidden off the roadside, the restaurant has an outdoor wooden deck that overlooks the downtown skyline and hosts a reggae band on weekends until the early hours of the morning. Fresh fish catches are listed on a chalkboard, but a meal could be made of the smoked-fish dip and conch-fritter appetizers. During dinner you may spot the rowing club working out in the cove; its headquarters is next door. On Friday and Sunday evenings **South Pointe Seafood House**, on the water's edge in South Pointe Park, provides front-row viewing of behemoth cruise ships trolling by on their way to or from the Caribbean. Live music on the outdoor patio on Friday nights tends to draw a younger, ferociously networking crowd (maybe it's the on-site microbrewery?). The food is unremarkable, far less outstanding than the views of the Cut, tony Fisher Island (former Vanderbilt digs), and the Atlantic Ocean.

Best-looking crowds... China Grill on South Beach is a cousin to the New York branch and just as noisy, popular, and chic. The dining room holds 200 diners, who all look like soap-opera actors or folks from a white-wine commercial. The menu is outstanding and the conversation level is manic. Try the lobster pancakes or the ground-lamb dumplings—foodies will rejoice. Black is the color of choice for the arty crowd at the **Starfish** restaurant on South Beach. Opened by an Armenian fashion maven, Starfish looks like a Manhattan transplant, but serves dishes that were inspired in the steamy tropics. The fashion-conscious crowd is fortunately uncloyingly hip and fun. They nibble lobster quesadillas with citrus salsa, and steamed yellowtail with roasted veggies. Make reservations, or else camp out at the bar and stargaze. On Wednesday nights there's a belly dancer and a Middle Eastern menu. Local-girl-made-glittery Gloria Estefan has an artistic hand in **Lario's on the Beach**, an upscale Cuban restaurant on Miami Beach's Ocean Drive. It's a jumping place, decorated in a funky Caribbean splash of color and textures with a faux blue sky that peeks out from above. The menu is traditional Cuban: roasted chicken, pork loin, side orders of fried bananas, and black beans and rice. The combo platter is a sampler from the Cuban-food welcome wagon, and a good introduction to yuca, plantains, and croquettes. Wash it all down with a *mojito*, a Cuban mint julep, and you're all the more likely to actually buy a Polaroid from the guy cruising the room selling candid moments. The clean and arid white walls of the **Century Cafe** in the Century Hotel on South Beach are broken only by pre-Columbian hanging decorations that look like little Rorschach tests. Though the menu offers an eclectic mix of Southwestern and Asian touches, fish is what the restaurant does best; the Cajun mahi mahi is the house specialty. Those who eschew meat can graze on appetizers like wild rice, garlic mashed potatoes, and spicy black beans.

People watching... Sooner or later, anyone who is anyone, or anyone who wants to be seen as anyone, passes by the **News Cafe**, a European-style cafe across the street from the ocean in South Beach. One of SoBe's oldest fixtures, the News is casual and chic, hip without trying to be. It's a great post-beach stop for lunch or for a light dinner of deli treats and veggie platters, even for an afternoon coffee while you scribble wish-you-were-here postcards to the crew back home. **Yuca**, a Cuban-moderne restaurant in Coral Gables (with a South Beach location, too), is one of the city's most popular locales for Nuevo Cubano food—things like plantains stuffed with beef, baby-back ribs braised in guava sauce, and mango flan so smooth it could double as face cream. The restaurant's name is a double entendre—a nod to the starchy standby side dish, as well as an acronym for the Young, Urban, Cuban-American crowd that hangs out here. You'll most likely spot repeated air kissing at **Caffè Baci**, a small Italian restaurant in Coral Gables. The decor—oversized vases with spidery flower arrangements against peach walls—is as understated as old money, which is what a lot of the sophisticated patrons seem to have. The Tuscan oven bakes fish and meat to a radiating tenderness, and the classic southern Italian dishes that round out the menu rely more on spices than sauces. Try tagliatelle pasta with porcini mushrooms, scallops sautéed in cognac and mustard, or seafood risotto. Perched on one of the busiest corners of Coconut Grove, **Green Street Cafe** has dozens of outdoor tables that provide front-row seats to the passing carnival: rickshaw drivers, jugglers and mimes, roving massage therapists, streetside musicians,

Bible thumpers threatening eternal damnation, gaggles of teens all dressed up with no place to show. Although it's billed as a gourmet French cafe, you'll be hard pressed to find anything approaching authentically Parisian. The salads are satisfying, though, and breakfast (the safest meal) is served into the night. You can also take in the Grove's dinnertime, Disney-esque mayhem from the second-story balcony perch of **Cafe Tu Tu Tango**. Located in the CocoWalk shopping center, this amiable restaurant is known for its array of tapas (which must be Spanish for "just enough to take the edge off your appetite"). Inside, the dim lighting throws shadows on walls ajumble with ragtag art.

Isn't it romantic?... Maybe it's the dusky courtyard on a Little Havana side street, maybe it's the Cuban antiques, or maybe it's the romantic piped-in sound track—whatever it is, the patrons at **Victor's Cafe** seem compelled to linger over their upscale tapas and entrées, and feed each another mouthfuls of their cassava turnover with lobster or their shrimp with yam quenelles. The well-heeled crowds are thickest here for Friday happy hour, but the later hours are best for trysting the night away. **Oggi Cafe** scores big with all that is romantically possible in an Italian restaurant. A discreet staff will look the other way during PDAs (public displays of affection). The crowd inside doesn't feel the need to advertise. And the decor won't compete with the object of your affection. It's all a bit understated at **Ristorante la Bussola**, a Coral Gables spot specializing in classically prepared Italian dishes. The interior echoes a Renaissance villa with umber-washed columns, brocades, and languid paintings of 15th-century musicians and artists. White tablecloths, piano music, couples leaning close in hushed conversation—you get the picture. Fettuccine with lobster and ravioli with white truffle sauce are house specialties. The ivy-covered **Restaurant St. Michel** has the feel and menu of an elegant Parisian cafe even though it's inside the Hotel Place St. Michel on one of Coral Gables' main arteries. Muted lighting from art-deco chandeliers, hardwood floors, brocade draperies, and top-drawer antiques make you feel as if you're in a countess's private dining room. The menu is a metropolitan melange of France and Florida, with entrees like yellowtail with fruit salsa and plantains, roasted duckling with tangy orange sauce, and venison and rabbit with citrus sauces.

Where Elvis would have eaten... Tucked onto feverishly commercial Washington Avenue, **Lulu's** is an oasis of kitsch and down-home cooking in a tongue-in-chic, two-story space that serves food somebody's Southern mama would have cooked for a Sunday supper: meat loaf and mashed potatoes, chicken-fried steak, rice pudding, and Elvis's purported fave snack, a fried peanut-butter-and-banana sandwich. The decor is high-camp, low-budget memorabilia pieced together from thrift stores and garage sales—Coke signs, old album covers, and Jetson-esque junque hung jauntily on the walls. Upstairs is a mini-Graceland shrine with Elvis photos, records, and assorted tchotchkes. The Road, as locals call the blues-hall-cum-bar-cum-burger-joint **Tobacco Road**, has the historic distinction of holding the oldest liquor license in Dade County (issued in 1912). Blues and funk bands perform in an upstairs space that was a speakeasy during Prohibition days. Downstairs, the narrow slice of a restaurant is decorated like someone's wood-paneled, circa-1978 den; thick happy-hour crowds jostle for space around the long wooden bar and among a handful of tables. Out back, a wooden deck holds chairs, umbrella-covered tables, and clusters of yuppies, construction workers, musicians, and after-work-ers. A mecca for outstanding bar food (Road burgers are mammoth) and a shot of low-rent fun. It's a flash of the fabulous fifties at **Allen's Drug Store**, a retro hangout in Coral Gables that serves Florida mom food like fried chicken, burgers, and, of course, slabs of genuine Key lime pie. Black-and-whites of bygone matinee idols adorn the walls, and a jukebox cranks out the kind of oldies everyone knows all the words to. Ten bucks says you're the only tourist in the place.

Cheap Italian eats... One of mid–Miami Beach's hidden treasures, **Cafe Prima Pasta** will never make it into *Architectural Digest,* but the food at this tiny restaurant with the less-is-more decor is consistently superb (far better than the budget prices would lead you to expect). The handmade pasta and first-class service keep them coming back for more. Arrive early to be assured a seat;

they don't take reservations. As close to a Tuscan trattoria as can be found anywhere in Miami, **da Leo Trattoria Toscano** is a convivial place where patrons cheerfully bump elbows as they munch bruschetta and twirl forkfuls of pasta. The food is sublime—the veal marsala and the tiramisu never miss—and the prices are some of the most reasonable among the glut of Italian restaurants that dot South Beach.

Cuban food... You can't really say you've sampled the flavor of Miami until you've had Cuban food. Heavy on the starches (and, many insist, the best cure for hangovers), *la comida Cubana* won't set off gastrointestinal warning bells the same way the spicier food of Mexico and Central America does. The lines that stream from **Islas Canarias**, a nondescript but ferociously popular Cuban restaurant on the industrial flatlands fringing downtown Miami, attest to the restaurant's reputation among exiles and gringos alike. Owned by the Garcia family, who hail from Tenerife in the Canary Islands, the menu is a melange of Cuban and Canary Island dishes. Though Islas has a second location in West Miami, this one draws the crowds, who eat traditional Cuban food and argue about Castro. For authentic Cuban food, **Versailles** has come to be a local institution. Try anything from the huge menu at this bustling, brightly lit restaurant in the heart of Little Havana. **La Carreta** on Calle Ocho is a boxy place that offers what Miami's Cuban restaurants are best known for: generous portions, quick service, and rib-sticking food. Select from an extensive and moderately priced menu of standards like *ropa vieja* (shredded roast beef in a light tomato sauce), *arroz con pollo* (chicken on a mound of yellow rice), or *picadillo* (ground beef seasoned with pimentos). For dessert, order the thick, woody café con leche and a flan. Tumble home to your hotel sated. (There are five locations around town, but the Calle Ocho one's the biggest and best.) Service is brusque, especially if English is your first language. Order by pointing—mangled Spanish doesn't go over too well here. The Spanish-influenced food served at **Malaga**, a hidden courtyard restaurant on Calle Ocho, will sate most carnivores on a budget. Vines and trees tangle against walls where time has streaked the paint; wooden tables make the courtyard feel like a jungle hideaway. A working knowledge of *español* will help here, but the wait staff won't mock you if you give it a go. Paella is one of the best dishes, but expect a long wait, since it's made to order.

Caribbean food... Miami is closer to Ocho Rios than it is to Boston, and the authentic tang of the languid Caribbean can be tasted at the **Marlin Bar** in the lobby of the Marlin Hotel on South Beach. Sit at one of the half-dozen front-porch tables, sipping a Red Stripe or a frothy rum drink accessorized with a plastic blue marlin, and wait for the dreadlocked waiters to serve you their specialty—the tangiest jerk chicken this side of Montego Bay. The funked-out decor blazes with the primary palette of the Caribbean. The **Tap Tap** Haitian restaurant on South Beach looks like a Caribbean art gallery: Sensuous images of Haitian village life dominate each of the dining rooms, and the tables and chairs are splashed with more colors than a big box of Crayolas. The authentic Haitian food is moderately priced and very spicy (despite what the waiter tells you).

Sushi... Locals know that light dinners help counterbalance the tropical heat, and there's not much that's lighter than a little miso soup and a little sushi. Inside the over-appliquéd and high-end Mayfair shopping center in Coconut Grove is **Chiyo Japanese Restaurant**. The deferential staff is garbed in authentic Japanese attire—it's like art in motion against the stark decor. A wraparound sushi bar and a teriyaki grill provide appetizers. The teriyaki dinners are the largest dishes, and the tempura dishes include a fried ice-cream dessert. Despite its name, which makes it sound like it has a severe case of the Hollywoods, South Beach's **Sushi Rock Cafe** is a relaxed, neighborhood Japanese restaurant peopled with regulars who all seem chummy with the sushi chef. This is veggie-ville: Stir-fried meatless dishes are just as tasty, though not as exotic, as the two dozen varieties of *makimono*.

Asian delights... Is the name a noun or a verb? At **Lure**, the artiest Asian restaurant on South Beach, it goes both ways: Burlap-covered lights are hung like lures from wooden fishing poles that hover over the tables; innovative East-West fusion food and a calmly sophisticated atmosphere have been luring diners back in ever-growing numbers. Pick from the list of entrées—half are fish—or put together a sampler of three or four of the appetizers like tempura shrimp with mango chutney or sesame seed–crusted tuna. The lack of trendiness at **Chrysanthemum**, a Chinese restaurant on South Beach, doesn't sap its energy or lower its desirability. Quite the contrary: This stylish restaurant serves Peking and Szechuan cooking in a quietly decorated dining room where diners aren't scanning the room to see who's better dressed. You've gotta try the flash-fried crispy spinach. For the stout of palate, order the five-alarm chicken with Szechuan peppers.

You say you've been dying for some alligator?... Burgers you can order anywhere, but good alligator, conch, or catfish (three of the area's indigenous goodies) are hard to find. To sample gator (yes, it does taste like chicken), go to the **Bimini Grill**, a casual slice of a restaurant on a canal just off the 79th Street Causeway, where you can get it either as a great appetizer in fried bite-size pieces, or as a munchie with a nice, cold draft beer. Alligator is also one of the selections on the tapas-only menu at the ever-boisterous **Cafe Tu Tu Tango** in the CocoWalk shopping center. For alligator with a dress code, mondo-opulent **Dominique's** in the oceanfront Alexander All-Suite Luxury Hotel in Miami Beach offers sautéed alligator tail as an appetizer. Here the reptile keeps company with other exotic selections like diamondback rattlesnake and buffalo sausage.

Cheap eats from south of the border... For the fiscally challenged but experimentally inclined, **El Inka** in the western reaches of the county is Miami's oldest Peruvian restaurant. Souvenirs of Peru are thumbtacked to the wall, plastic covers floral tablecloths, and the mismatched crockery conjures up adjectives like rustic, genuine, and unpretentious. The ceviches are memorable, especially the Inka Special, which is swimming with octopus, sea bass, squid, clams, and scallops. A meat-and-potato stew called *seco de res* should take care of the John Waynes in your group. In the midst of the high hemlines, high prices, and high jinks of South Beach, **Puerto Sagua** is an anachronism: A three-sided counter with stools fills one room, and laminated wooden tables cluster in another. On the walls are original dioramas of Cuban street life by the two Scull sisters, expats who now call the Beach home. P.S., as the locals call it, is where you'll find Cubanos seeking authentic *comidas*, hipsters who lurch in to quell late-night munchies, and budget-conscious backpackers who drift in from the nearby youth hostel.

Where the portions are larger than Montana...
The best of the Indian restaurants in Miami, **House of India** serves spicy curries, kabobs, and tandoori in oversize portions. The acidic hum of Indian music plays in the background, and Indian wall hangings and wooden screens decorate this understated, bi-level restaurant. Heed your server's advice about the spices or you may end up with a four-alarm dinner. It's a meat-fest amid swordplay at **Rodeo Grill**, an upscale Brazilian restaurant in Coral Gables. The name of the restaurant is an anglicized version of the name of their trademark specialty, *rodizio,* a stupefyingly filling combo of spit-roasted pork, chicken, turkey, lamb, and ribs. The confirmed carnivores who order this dish get a rodeo show along with their grill: This prix-fixe parade of meats is trotted to your plate by swashbuckling waiters. A buffet offers vegetables and salads as side dishes.

For sports fans... Decorated in a locker-room-shrine motif, with photos from Johnson's coaching career papering the walls of the glass-enclosed dining room, it's TV-o-rama at **Jimmy Johnson's Three Rings Bar & Grill**. Thirty-eight televisions, including two mondo 12-foot screens, blast sports from every angle (it's quieter on the oceanside deck). Though the menu calls itself Floribbean (a hybrid of Florida and Caribbean), roaring for the hometown team goes best with one of the football-sized burgers. The European crowd that frequents **Sport Cafe** prefers having the restaurant's four televisions tuned to soccer or tennis rather than football. Although there are tables on the front sidewalk for people watching, most of the action is inside this low-key Washington Avenue restaurant, where patrons wear shorts, the waiters look harried, and five or six languages mingle in the air with the smell of garlic and sweat. The sparse menu relies heavily on pasta—the daily specials are always a sure bet. And the bar is where the fanatics gather, trading trivia and slamming down brews and carafes of the house red wine.

Best-looking crowds in docksiders... Water, water everywhere, and here's the place to drink. **Monty's Bayshore Restaurant** on Biscayne Bay in Coconut Grove is really three places in one: There's an inside lounge for the more sedate, and an indoor restaurant that serves competent surf-and-turf food, but the real draw is the dockside bar with its live music, live crowd, and whiff of salt breezes. Seafood finger foods like raw oysters, conch fritters, and stone crabs will cure the munchies. **Sunday's on the Bay** feels like a nautically themed frat party in the Virgin Islands rather than a restaurant bar on Key Biscayne, the spit of land where Richard Nixon often wintered. It's usually tanned elbow to tanned elbow with fishermen, boaties, tourists sporting pink noses, and those who think dressing up means donning a fresh T-shirt. Seafood and rum are the top sellers. Reggae music and conviviality reign Thursday through Sunday nights.

The Index

$$$$	over $20
$$$	$15–$20
$$	$10–$15
$	under $10

Prices reflect average price of dinner; drinks and tip not included.

Allen's Drug Store. It's time-warp city in this Coral Gables drugstore where you half expect Archie and Veronica to take the table behind you. Mom-and-Pop food rules here, but don't skip the Key lime pie (it's the real thing).... *Tel 305/ 666–8581. 4000 Red Rd., Miami. Reservations not accepted. $*

Astor Place. Muted tones in a glass atrium in this intimate and stylish new restaurant on Washington Avenue in the thick of SoBe action. This is carnivore central, but the menu is balanced by lighter selections like sandwiches and ample salads.... *Tel 305/672–7217. Astor Hotel, 956 Washington Ave., Miami Beach. Reservations required. $$*

Bayside Hut. The best time for the Hut, as locals call it, is sunset, when the downtown skyline glows with neon. Conch fritters, fish sandwiches, and smoked-fish dip so smoky it'll make your crackers weep.... *Tel 305/361–0808. 3501 Rickenbacker Causeway, Key Biscayne. Reservations not accepted. $*

Biltmore Courtyard Cafe. This restaurant is inside one of the city's most beautiful buildings, worthy of a pilgrimage in itself. The Sunday brunch is elegant and plentiful. On Tuesday nights an opera singer serenades your table. The salads are inventive and the fish dishes are fine.... *Tel 305/445–1926, ext. 1820. Biltmore Hotel, 1200 Anastasia Ave., Coral Gables. $$–$$$*

Bimini Grill. This seafood shack, fronting on a canal in northern Miami, looks as if it belongs in Key West. The jukebox plays country tunes and the large, lit patio out back is dotted with nets and buoys as decor. Alligator is a favorite appetizer.... *Tel 305/758–9154. 620 NE 78th St., Miami. Reservations not accepted. No credit cards. $*

Blue Door. High fashion and high drama at South Beach's hottest restaurant. Co-owned by Madonna and frequented by stars, models, and celebs who munch on continental standards with a tropical twist. A must-see for the glamorously inclined.... *Tel 305/674–6400. Delano Hotel, 1685 Collins Ave., Miami Beach. Reservations required. $$$*

Cafe Prima Pasta. Nobody flocks to this small Miami Beach Italian restaurant for the decor. But they do come and they wait because they know the homemade pasta is hard to beat. The budget prices don't hurt either.... *Tel 305/867–0106. 414 71st St., Miami Beach. Reservations not accepted. No credit cards. $*

Cafe Tu Tu Tango. This lively tapas restaurant in the CocoWalk shopping center is always crowded, especially on the second-story outdoor patio, which offers great views of the wacky street life of downtown Coconut Grove. Open Friday and Saturday nights to 2am.... *Tel 305/529–2222. CocoWalk, 3015 Grand Ave., Coconut Grove. Reservations not accepted. $$*

Caffè Baci. A gold vaulted ceiling makes this narrow place seem larger than it is and sets off the quiet fabulousness of the hopelessly sophisticated crowd sipping San Pelligrino. The kitchen draws most of its inspiration from southern Italy—spices and subtle seasonings, less sauce.... *Tel 305/442–0600. 2522 Ponce de Leon Blvd., Coral Gables. Reservations recommended. $$$*

Caffè Milano. You may end up eating next to Mel Brooks or Robin Williams or Cindy Crawford at this self-consciously hip

Italian restaurant in the heart of the South Beach scene.... *Tel 305/532–0707. 850 Ocean Dr., Miami Beach. Reservations required. $$$*

Century Cafe. No larger than a cafe, this is a decidedly quiet place where fashion types and writers—staying at the Century Hotel—like to congregate. They sit in the shadows of the pre-Columbian art and select from the entrées that fuse Asia with the American Southwest.... *Tel 305/674–8855. 140 Ocean Dr., Miami Beach. Reservations recommended for dinner. $$$–$$$$*

Chart House. At the lovely, sedate Coconut Grove entry in this national chain, parked next to the Dinner Key Marina, fish is the draw, though the prime rib and filet mignon barely need a knife. The views of the bay and Miami Beach beyond are romantic.... *Tel 305/856–9741. 51 Chart House Dr., Coconut Grove. $$*

Chef Allen's Restaurant. The black-lacquer chairs and glass-block and hot-pink neon interior may make you feel as if you're in a "Miami Vice" rerun, but Allen Susser's Floribbean menu is up-to-date and inventive.... *Tel 305/935–2900. 19088 NE 29th Ave., North Miami Beach. Reservations required. $$–$$$*

China Grill. This bustling, 200-seat, au courant South Beach restaurant is cousin to eatery of the same name in New York. And like its kin, the clientele is equally beautiful, international, and pores over menus of inventive pan-Asian food.... *Tel 305/534–2211. 404 Washington Ave., Miami Beach. Reservations required. $$$$*

Chiyo Japanese Restaurant. Shoppers from the upscale Mayfair and nearby CocoWalk shopping centers like to duck in here for a chair at the sushi bar.... *Tel 305/445–0865. Mayfair Shops in the Grove, 3399 Virginia St., Coconut Grove. Reservations not accepted. $$*

Chrysanthemum. If it weren't for the Chinese artwork, it would be difficult to tell that this sophisticated, dinner-only South Beach restaurant serves uptown Peking and Szechuan dishes. The crispy duck with five flavors borders on a religious experience.... *Tel 305/531–5656. 1256*

Washington Ave., Miami Beach. Dinner only. Reservations recommended. $$$

Colony Bistro. This place is abuzz with energy and innovative dishes that combine at least four foods of the moment. A chatty bar on the second floor overlooks the dining room below, which features both indoor and outdoor seating.... *Tel 305/673–0088. 736 Ocean Dr., Miami Beach. Reservations recommended. $$$*

da Leo Trattoria Toscana. The authenticity starts with the Italian waiters and trickles down to the pasta dishes and the veal marsala that has become the house specialty.... *Tel 305/674–0350. 819 Lincoln Rd., Miami Beach. Reservations recommended. $*

Dominique's. The lights from ocean liners twinkle in the distance, making the views from this (slightly eccentric) French restaurant on Miami Beach as seductive as the nouvelle wizardry performed in its kitchen. Treat yourself to something exotic like sautéed alligator tail, or stick to the more traditional bistro fare.... *Tel 305/861–5252. Alexander All-Suite Luxury Hotel, 5225 Collins Ave., Miami Beach. Reservations recommended. Jackets required for men. $$$$*

East Coast Fisheries. Sit outside at one of the riverside tables and order the conch fritters as a warm-up to the catch of the night—anything from bluefish, grouper, or flounder to stone crabs or dolphin fish.... *Tel 305/372–1300. 360 W. Flagler St., Miami. Reservations not accepted. $$*

El Inka. With a menu that offers traditional Peruvian food and waitresses eager to talk about the motherland, Miami's oldest Peruvian restaurant is worth the drive. Sample the excellent house ceviche and the chartreuse-colored Inka cola.... *Tel 305/553–4074. 11049 SW 40th St., Miami. Reservations not accepted. $*

A Fish Called Avalon. An elegant restaurant on the hippest street around. Locals flock to the sidewalk tables for views of the ocean and night sky, and some stunning people-watching opportunities. And the fish ain't bad, either.... *Tel*

305/532–1727. 700 Ocean Dr., Miami Beach. Reservations recommended. $$$

The Forge. The word *ornate* takes on new meaning in this mid-Beach restaurant that does everything over the top. Meat's the name of the game—the kitchen does best with beef, veal, and duck—and the wine list is the city's longest. The service is predictably officious and the dress code leans toward ascots and sequins.... *Tel 305/538–8533. 432 41st St., Miami Beach. Reservations required. Jackets required for men. $$$$*

Gourmet Diner. The name of this north Miami restaurant is really not an oxymoron. Professors from nearby universities, other locals, and occasional errant snowbirds regularly fill up the banquettes and the counter to dine on the mostly French entrées.... *Tel 305/947–2255. 13951 Biscayne Blvd., North Miami Beach. Reservations not accepted. No credit cards. $$*

Green Street Cafe. The in-the-middle-of-it-all location of this Coconut Grove sidewalk restaurant is what packs the tables, not the so-so food or the often inattentive service. Use this as a late-night munchie stop. Open weekends until 1am.... *Tel 305/567–0662. 3110 Commodore Plaza, Coconut Grove. Reservations not accepted. $*

House of India. Is there such a thing as down-home Indian food? This must be it. The portions are consistently huge, especially the tandoori dishes.... *Tel 305/444–2348. 22 Merrick Way, Coral Gables. Reservations not accepted. $–$$*

Hy Vong. Incongruously situated in the midst of Little Havana, this unpretentious, 36-seat Vietnamese restaurant is best visited before 7pm if you want to avoid the line for a table. Pick from the United Nations list of beers to help extinguish the spiciness of authentic dishes like fish pan-fried in lime-garlic sauce or barbecued pork with sesame seeds.... *Tel 305/446–3674. 3458 SW 8th St., Miami. Dinner only. Reservations not accepted. No credit cards. $$*

Islas Canarias. This nondescript Cuban favorite is frequented by exiled writers, artists, and thinkers. The food is plentiful and traditional.... *Tel 305/649–0440, 285 NW 27th Ave., Miami; tel 305/559–6666, 13685 Coral Way, Miami. Reservations not accepted. No credit cards.* $

Jimmy Johnson's Three Rings Bar & Grill. Named after the Dolphins' new head coach, this memorial to the locker room has a good number of tropical Floribbean entrées on its menu, though most of the jocks (and ex-jocks) come for the beer and burgers, and nonstop sports on the oversized TVs. And although you won't be able to see much of it, the ocean is just short yardage from the outdoor patio tables.... *Tel 305/672–6224. Eden Roc Resort, 4525 Collins Ave., Miami Beach. Reservations not accepted.* $$

Joe's Stone Crab. This Miami legend bustles with informality. No reservations means lines snake around the block as salivating patrons wait their turn for the house special of stone-crab claws, hash browns, creamed spinach, and Key lime pie. For those who don't want to wait, Joe's Take Away is right next door.... *Tel 305/673–0365 (tel 305/673–4611 for Joe's Stone Crab Take Away). 227 Biscayne Blvd., Miami Beach. Reservations not accepted.* $$$

La Carreta. A Cuban favorite, heavy on the meat and potatoes, and light on the wallet. Open 24/7.... *Tel 305/444–7501. 3632 SW 8th St., Miami, and other locations. Reservations not accepted.* $

Lario's on the Beach. Yuppie Cuban food is what they're ordering at this busy Gloria Estefan–financed restaurant on South Beach. Order a *mojito* (Cuban rum-and-tonic speckled with crushed mint leaves) and the sampler platter as an intro to cuisine Cubano.... *Tel 305/532–9577. 820 Ocean Dr., Miami Beach. Reservations not accepted.* $$

Le Sandwicherie. Baguette sandwiches are taken out—mostly in the wee, post-clubbing hours—from this curbside South Beach shop no bigger than a closet. The clientele here— many from the divey bar across the street or from the adjacent tattoo parlor—look as if they just walked out of a Mary Ellen Mark photo essay. Open until 5am daily.... *Tel 305/ 532–8934. 229 14th St., Miami Beach. Reservations not accepted.* $

MIAMI ☾ **LATE NIGHT DINING**

Lulu's. Southern comfort food, like meat loaf and fried chicken with mashed potatoes, are scarfed up here in the midst of kitschy thrift-shop decor. A favorite of South Beachers looking for affordable, no-frills food. Don't leave without making a pilgrimage to the Elvis shrine upstairs.... *Tel 305/532–6147. 1053 Washington Ave., Miami Beach. Reservations not accepted. $*

Lure. At this trendy Asian restaurant on South Beach's Lincoln Road Mall, burlap-covered lights hang like lures from wooden fishing poles suspended above the goldfish that swim in bowls on each table.... *Tel 305/538–5873. 805 Lincoln Rd., Miami Beach. Reservations recommended. $$$*

Malaga. Charmingly decayed and aged by the elements. Regulars phone ahead with their paella order, and know that the pot roast cooked with veal, sausages, and pork will require a doggie bag.... *Tel 305/858–4224. 740 SW 8th St., Miami. Reservations not accepted. $*

Mark's Place. Visiting celebs and shakers sooner or later end up at this sophisticated and unmistakably urban bistro plunked in the middle of an innocuous North Miami shopping center. Celebrity chef Mark Militello's Floribbean inventions include black grouper encased in a pistachio crust, and oak-roasted salmon.... *Tel 305/893–6888. 2286 NE 123rd St., North Miami. Reservations required for dinner. $$$*

Marlin Bar. The big item at this Jamaican spot (formerly the Shabeen Cookshack): the jerk chicken appetizers. A cross-section of South Beachers gathers to sip rum drinks, shoot pool, or meet friends in this hyperfunky indoor-outdoor spot... *Tel 305/673–8373. Marlin Hotel, 1200 Collins Ave., Miami Beach. Reservations not accepted. $*

Monty's Bayshore Restaurant. Crowds flock to the dockside bar of this Grove institution, where a Jimmy Buffett ethos prevails. A frisky crowd drinks longnecks while swaying to live reggae music; things can get a little rowdy.... *Tel 305/858–1431. 2550 S. Bayshore Dr., Coconut Grove. Reservations recommended. $$*

Nemo. Nouvelle organic food is shuttled to artfully designed tables and coolly chic patrons who come garbed in post-beach pareos and little linen numbers.... *Tel 305/532–4550. 100 Collins Ave., Miami Beach. Reservations recommended. $$*

News Cafe. Conceived in the European sidewalk-cafe mold, the News is a place where everyone—locals and visitors—should end up either sipping a latte or picking at a sandwich while ogling a live, nocturnal, flesh-and-flash parade that's better than any of the print versions in the fashion mags for sale inside.... *Tel 305/538–6397. 800 Ocean Dr., Miami Beach. Reservations not accepted. $*

Oggi Cafe. Tables edge so close to each other at this out-of-the-way Italian restaurant (run by a triumvirate of Argentineans—who knew?) that strangers strike up conversations with the regulars, most of whom recommend the tri-pasta sampler and a bottle of red.... *Tel 305/866–1238. 1740 79th St. Causeway, North Bay Village. Reservations not accepted. $*

Osteria del Teatro. Italian restaurants on South Beach come and go like fads, but Osteria has held fast. Maybe it's because of the reliably irresistible salmon stuffed with crabmeat and shrimp, or the fish with pancetta and marinated eggplant.... *Tel 305/538–7850. 1443 Washington Ave., Miami Beach. Reservations required (often weeks in advance). $$$*

Pacific Time. Under the direction of Jonathan Eismann, one of South Florida's hotshot chefs, the menu here is "Asian-influenced American food with a French head." That translates into things like Peking pancakes or grilled squid with Asian greens and hot-and-sour vinaigrette. The glamour quotient peaks at about 11pm.... *Tel 305/534–5979. 915 Lincoln Rd., Miami Beach. Reservations recommended. $$$*

Puerto Sagua. The best neighborhood black-beans-and-rice restaurant on South Beach slings platters of wallet-friendly Cuban standards in two rooms filled with older Cubanos, the terminally hip, street people, backpackers, and turistas. The 75-cent *cafecito* (Cuban espresso) is akin to jet fuel.... *Tel 305/673–1115. 700 Collins Ave., Miami Beach. Reservations not accepted. $*

Raleigh Restaurant & Bar. The terrazzo floors, Billie Holiday sound track, and flicker-dim lighting lend a muted forties sophistication to the New American cuisine served here. Try for the patio: It overlooks a certifiably authentic Florida-scape complete with palm-encircled pool and the great, dark Atlantic beyond.... *Tel 305/534–1775. Raleigh Hotel, 1775 Collins Ave., Miami Beach. Reservations required. $$$*

Rascal House. Folklore has it that more than 5,000 customers move through this Jewish deli and restaurant every day, a good number of them after dark. The menu has all the classics, including pastrami and corned-beef sammies, brisket, and a coma-inducing lemon pie. Open until 1am on Saturday and Sunday.... *Tel 305/947–4581. 17190 Collins Ave., Miami Beach. Reservations not accepted. No credit cards. $*

Restaurant St. Michel. While cell phones and briefcases rest on tabletops here by day, by night romance is the only deal-making done in this hotel restaurant. The grilled veal steak with mustard-peppercorn sauce is rumored to have aphrodisiacal powers.... *Tel 305/446–6572. Place St. Michel Hotel, 162 Alcazar Ave., Coral Gables. Reservations recommended. $$$*

Ristorante la Bussola. Always included in the roundups of outstanding Italian restaurants, La Bussola prides itself on its Renaissance decor, its attentive service, and its classically prepared entrées.... *Tel 305/445–8783. 264 Giralda Ave., Coral Gables. Reservations recommended. $$$*

Rodeo Grill. Flashes of Zorro at this Coral Gables Brazilian restaurant: Entertaining waiters serve your meat skewered on their swords. It's a first-class food-fest and a mecca for business types with carnivorous cravings in the post-work hours.... *Tel 305/447–6336. 2121 Ponce de Leon Blvd., Coral Gables. Reservations recommended. $$$*

Rusty Pelican. The wide, electric skyline of downtown Miami makes this chain seafood house one of the most seductive spots in the city. Warm up by sharing a margarita (or two) at sunset with the affable swarm of humanity at the bar.... *Tel 305/361–3818. 3201 Rickenbacker Causeway, Key*

Biscayne. Reservations recommended, especially for waterside tables. $$

Scotty's Landing. You'll see mostly T-shirts and flip-flops here, though a few suits loosening their ties usually sniff out this backyard bayside seafood spot next to the Dinner Key Marina. You can't go wrong ordering the reliably fresh fish sandwich or a bowl of fish soup crowned with crushed saltines.... *Tel 305/854–2626. 3381 Pan American Dr., Coconut Grove. Reservations not accepted. $*

South Pointe Seafood House. Snag an outside table at this restaurant-microbrewery on the southernmost tip of Miami Beach at sunset and you'll think you've landed in some Floridean version of Fellini's *Amarcord;* the cruise ships gliding by seem close enough to touch. At night you can see the lights of chi-chi Fisher Island in one direction and the downtown skyline in the other.... *Tel 305/673–1708. 1 Washington Ave., Miami Beach. Reservations recommended. $$*

Sport Cafe. Despite all its tony neighbors, this small Italian restaurant on South Beach is unpretentious and *almost* budget-priced. The daily pasta dishes are always fresh and reliable. Though there are sidewalk tables, there's more action inside, where a young crowd is usually rallying around a televised soccer game.... *Tel 305/674–9700. 538 Washington Ave., Miami Beach. Reservations not accepted. $*

Starfish. In the only section of South Beach where you can still score on-street parking with little hassle, this quietly upscale, candlelit restaurant caters to transplanted Manhattanites, the fashion-industry crowd, and assorted hipsters. Hamburgers and meat loaf meet lobster quesadillas and salmon carpaccio.... *Tel 305/673–1717. 1427 West Ave., Miami Beach. Reservations required. $$$*

Sundays on the Bay. A piece of the Caribbean on Key Biscayne, Sunday's is a waterfront, good-time place. Seafood's the thing, and weekend reggae bands on Sunday nights until 1am attract a rum-drinking crowd in shorts and suntans.... *Tel 305/361–6777. 5420 Crandon Blvd., Key Biscayne. $$*

Sushi Rock Cafe. Stick to the sushi at this neighborhood Japanese restaurant; it's really what it does best. The location, at the epicenter of South Beach, makes it a prime stop either for dinner or a healthy post-club nosh.... *Tel 305/ 532–2133. 1351 Collins Ave., Miami Beach. Reservations not accepted. $$$*

Tap Tap. Startling, vivid scenes of Haitian life electrify the walls of this casual South Beach restaurant. The Caribbean menu features classics of the region like goat, meat patties, and jerk chicken.... *Tel 305/672–2898. 819 5th St., Miami Beach. Reservations not accepted. $$*

Tobacco Road. This bar, blues hall, and burger joint is free of posers and heavy on regulars who come to munch down Road burgers in their many high-cholesterol variations. Happy hour is yuppie time. Open until 5am seven days a week.... *Tel 305/374–1198. 626 S. Miami Ave., Miami. Reservations not accepted. $*

Van Dyke Cafe. Bistro food is served 24 hours a day at this prime people-watching spot on South Beach's Lincoln Road pedestrian mall. The salads, pastas, soups, and sandwiches are on the health-conscious side. A word of warning: They automatically add 15% of your bill for a tip.... *Tel 305/534– 3600. 1641 Jefferson Ave., Miami Beach. Reservations not accepted. $–$$*

Versailles. Multi-tiered pastry houses rotate in the corners of this overlit Cuban carnival of a restaurant, one of the city's must-sees. Huge portions of standard Cuban fare are served until the wee hours amidst a bustling, bilingual buzz. Open until 2am Monday-Thursday, 3:30am on Friday night, and 4:30am Saturday and Sunday..... *Tel 305/ 444–0240. 3555 SW 8th St., Miami. Reservations not accepted. $*

Victor's Cafe. Decorated in the colonial style of Old Havana, this cafe (which has a sister restaurant in New York) is known for its stylish patrons and such expertly prepared Cuban food as stone crabs Creole and black-bean soup.... *Tel 305/445–1313. 2340 SW 32nd Ave., Miami. Reservations required. $$–$$$*

Wolfie's. A classic Jewish deli, circa 1963. The waitresses offer advice and crown each table with a gratis plate of mini-danishes and a bowl of fat pickles. The gooey blintzes are a sure thing. Open all day, every day.... *Tel 305/538–6626. 2038 Collins Ave., Miami Beach. Reservations not accepted.* $

Yuca. Nuevo Cubano cuisine, one of Miami's own inventions, is served in this sleek restaurant.... *Tel 305/532–9822. 501 Lincoln Rd., Miami Beach. Reservations recommended on weekends.* $$$

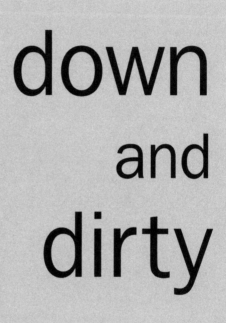

down
and
dirty

Airports... About six miles west of downtown, Miami International Airport is a standard-issue, ultramodern international airport—its concourses bustle with all the usual overpriced souvenir shops, boutiques, bars, restaurants, and services. The seventh-largest international airport in the U.S., MIA is a major stop for carriers that service Central and South America; in some of the waiting areas you'll feel as if you're at a meeting of the Organization of American States.

Airport transportation... To find transportation, exit Miami International Airport on the lower concourse, near the baggage claim area. **Taxis** are the fastest way to get where you're going. They charge flat fees to and from the airport, costing about $22 for a 15-minute ride to downtown Miami Beach. Locals and tourists hop on the more economical **SuperShuttle** (tel 305/871–2000 in Miami; 800/874–8885 from outside Florida), the big blue vans with mustard-yellow lettering. A one-way trip to Coral Gables, for example, runs about $14–$20; to the Art Deco District in South Beach, about $10. Since you have to wait your turn to be dropped off at your hotel, the vans take twice as long as cabs, but you can sit back and relax and catch some slices of Miami. To return to the airport on the shuttle, make a reservation at least 24 hours in advance of your departure. **Metrobuses** ($1.25 fare with 25¢ transfers), part of Miami's public transportation system, are another option, but they often run late and are inconvenient. They leave once every hour from the arrivals area on the upper concourse of the airport, and don't offer direct connections to hotels and resort areas.

All-night pharmacies... Several **Walgreens** pharmacies (In Miami Beach, tel 305/531–8868, 1845 Alton Rd.; in North Miami, tel 305/893–7093; 12295 Biscayne Blvd.) are open 24 hours, seven days a week. Both locations listed also have adjacent liquor stores under the same management that stay open until the wee hours.

Babysitters... Most large hotels have listings of licensed and insured babysitters available at the concierge desk, or call **Lul-A-Bye Sitters Registry** (tel 305/565–1222), a reputable local firm licensed and insured with sitters of all ages for babies and children of all ages.

Car rentals... If you didn't drive your car to town you're probably going to need to rent one. Miami is spread out, and the public transportation system is not an efficient way to get around, especially at night. However, if you'll be spending the whole time in South Beach you won't need a car, since it's easy enough to walk around and hail a cab if you get tired. Dozens of car-rental companies are found here, from the major chains to local Mom-and-Pop places where you can get a car for less than $100 a week. The biggies are: **Alamo** (tel 800/327–9633), **Avis** (tel 800/331–1212), **Budget** (tel 800/527–0700), **Hertz** (tel 800/654–9887), and **National** (tel 800/328–4567). A cheapo local company is **Titan Rent-A-Car** (tel 305/266–5133). Remember: Local thugs hone in on tourists who drive rental cars. Lock everything in your trunk—even when you're driving—and don't drive with a map in your hands. If you do, you might as well have the word "tourist" tattooed on your forehead.

Credit cards.... **American Express** offices are located at 14261 Commerce Way, Miami Lakes. If you left home without it, or if your card is lost or stolen, call 800/528–4800. If someone swipes your **MasterCard** call 800/826–2181, and if they get the **Visa** try 800/336–8472.

Crime tips... If you rent a car, avoid getting one that advertises itself as a rental. Most rental companies no longer plaster bumper stickers with their company logo on their vehicles, but check yours out, just to be sure. Also, keep your rental-car contract tucked out of sight.

There are several seedy and dangerous neighborhoods nestled between the airport and the tourist destinations of Miami Beach, Coconut Grove, and Coral Gables. If you get lost or miss your exit, stay on the state road and follow the **orange sunburst signs**. They will lead you to tourist-friendly areas, where you can stop and ask for directions. If a car behind you flashes its lights, as if in distress, don't pull over. This is a common robbery ploy, targeted at tourists. Follow your instincts and stay alert. For more safety tips and information, tune into **102.3 FM**, a 24-hour broadcast of tourist news broadcast in English, Spanish, French, and German.

Doctors... For a referral, call the **Physicians' Referral Service** (tel 305/324-8717) or the **University of Miami Physicians' Referral Office** (tel 305/547-5757). Based on your symptoms, they'll refer you to the appropriate MD. **The East Coast Dental Society** (tel 305/667–

3647) is available 24 hours daily, to provide a list of around-the-clock dental services.

Driving around... Driving can be fun, or a nightmare, or a combination of both. If you have a convertible, work it: Soak up the sun and ride with the wind. Seeing all of the city's major tourist spots means you'll have to navigate the big roads—expressways and interstates—and potential traffic jams. In the morning rush, a large flood of commuters rolls north and east into downtown. In the late afternoons, those folks head back south and west. Avoid driving north on I-95 from 7:30 to 9:30am and south from 4 to 6pm. Local radio stations give up-to-the-minute morning, afternoon, and late-afternoon traffic-crunch reports. For more roadway information, call **Florida Road Conditions** (tel 305/470–5349). Some road rules: Every passenger must don a seatbelt; you can turn right on red after stopping; and don't flip the finger at other drivers if they cut you off; in this town they *really* might cut you off—for good!

Emergencies... For an ambulance, paramedic, police, or fire rescue, dial **911**. Other emergency services are listed on the front inside cover of Miami telephone books. Major hospitals with reputable emergency rooms are: **Baptist Hospital** (305/596–6556), **Mercy Hospital** (tel 305/285–2171), **Miami Heart Institute** (tel 305/672–1111), and **Mount Sinai Medical Center** (tel 305/674–2121). Hotlines include: **The Abuse Registry** (tel 800/962–2873), **Coast Guard Search & Rescue** (tel 305/535–4314), the **Florida Poison Information Center** (tel 800/282–3171), and the **Rape Hotline** (tel 305/585–7273).

Festivals and special events...

January: **Art Deco Weekend** (tel 305/672–2014; Ocean Dr., between 5th and 16th Sts.; second or third weekend in Jan.) is a festival filled with lectures, exhibits, and art celebrating this 20th-century pastel-colored architecture.

February: For some reel fun try **The Miami Film Festival** (tel 305/377–3456, Gusman Theater and other screening rooms; first week of February), a big draw for celebrities, on opening night at least. Latin lovebird Antonio Banderas and wife, Melanie Griffith, graced the 1996 festival. Call months in advance for tickets; they are available through either Ticketmaster or the Gusman Center box office. **Coconut Grove Arts Festival** (tel 305/447–0410, streets of downtown

Coconut Grove; mid-February) is a mega–outdoor arts extravaganza along the city streets which kicks off in the morning and runs into the evening. **Taste of the Grove** (tel 305/444–7270; Peacock Park, Coconut Grove; mid-February) is a giant food fest in the bohemian hub of Miami.

March: **Carnaval Miami** (tel 305/644–8888; Little Havana; week before Lent), the annual weeklong festival of Cuban food, art, crafts, and culture culminates in the **Calle Ocho Festival** (on the last weekend before Lent), where hordes of people strut their stuff in a giant conga line that, from the air, looks like a Cuban centipede.

April: **Merrick Festival** (tel 305/447-9299; Circle Park, Coral Gables; second weekend in April) is a celebration of the performing arts, featuring opera, theatre, dance and music.

May: The **Subtropics Music Festival**, sponsored by the Cultura del Lobo (tel 305/758–6676; various venues around town; second week of May) offers an array of musical performances from non-commercial artists, including chamber music, electronic music, multimedia installations, and dance performances, many of which are free of charge.

June: **Goombay Festival** (tel 305/444–7270; Grand Ave., Coconut Grove; second weekend in June), is a three-day-long festivity paying tribute to Bahamian culture. Hear island music and dance your pants off.

July: **Fourth of July fireworks** (tel 305/577–3344; 401 Biscayne Blvd.), at Bayside Market Place, sends blasts and blares over Miami's downtown skyline.

August: At the **Reggae Festival** (tel 305/891–2944; AT&T Amphitheatre, 301 Biscayne Blvd., downtown Miami; first weekend in August) you'll hear an assortment of bands from Jamaica.

September: **Festival Miami** (tel 305/284–3941; Maurice Gusman Concert Hall, UM campus; early September through late October) is classical-music concerts, plays, and art-gallery presentations sponsored by the University of Miami.

October: **Saturday and Sunday in the Park with Art** (tel 305/238–0703; Fairchild Tropical Gardens, Miami; third weekend in October) is an opportunity for local artists to display their masterpieces.

November: **Miami Book Fair International** (tel 305/237–3258; Miami Dade Community College; third week of November) is a four-day festival for book worms, buffs, authors, and just plain books.

December: **King Mango Strut** (tel 305/444–7270; Coconut Grove; Dec. 29) spoofs the annual Orange Bowl Parade, with a zany cast of characters strolling through Coconut Grove in floats. Past players: The Unabombers; Hugh Grant and Divine Brown impersonators; and The Grateful Freds, who pay tribute to the Grateful Dead. **Orange Bowl Parade** (tel 305/371–4600; Biscayne Blvd.; Dec. 31) Watch King Orange roll down Biscayne Boulevard with national high school marching bands tooting their horns.

Gay and lesbian resources... Gay and lesbian news and views are featured in the **"twn"**section of the *Weekly News.* It's free and distributed in stores and mailboxes in Coconut Grove and South Beach. Lesbians may want to peek into *She Times*, a free, monthly rag with news in English and Spanish. **The Gay & Lesbian Hotline** (tel 305/759–3661) is a recorded message about gay events and services.

Miscellaneous resources... Other helpful numbers include: **AIDS Hotline** (tel 800/342–2437), **Better Business Bureau** (tel 305/625–0307), **Elder Helpline** (tel 305/670–4357), **Information and Referral Hotline for Community Service Organizations** (tel 305/358–4357), and **Hearing Impaired Services** (tel and TDD 305/668–4407).

Movie hotline... For the latest movies playing in Dade's movie houses, call **Moviephone** (tel 305/888–3456). You can also buy tickets ahead of time with this service and a credit card.

Newspapers and magazines... Stroll into a bar, pub, bookstore, or coffeehouse and chances are you'll run into a stack of weeklies, newspapers, and magazines. The best source of local and national news in South Florida is *The Miami Herald*, touted for its daily coverage of Central and South America. On Fridays, look at the paper's "Weekend" section for information about galleries, movies, concerts, and clubs. For celebrity sightings and club gossip, check out Tara Solomon's "Queen of the Night" column inside. *El Nuevo Herald* is *The Miami*

Herald's Spanish daily that comes free inside the English edition. *New Times* is a free, alternative weekly published on Thursdays. The thick personal ad section makes for fun reading. Two local magazines that most visitors pick up on the way to the beach are *South Florida*, a glossy arts-and-entertainment rag for folks with *mucho* time and *mucho* dough, and *Ocean Drive Magazine*, geared toward South Beach's fashion, faces, celebrities, and happenings. A little weekly called *Wire* gives the latest club updates for South Beach.

Opening and closing times... Most businesses downtown are open from 9 to 5 Monday through Saturday. Shopping malls are generally open seven days a week and stay open until 9 or 10pm. Businesses in Coconut Grove and South Beach tend to stay open a bit later to accommodate those party-animal residents and visitors for whom sundown is the middle of the day.

Parking... It's either on-street, garage, or metered parking in South Beach. Bring tons of change if you're going to park at a meter: They're constantly hungry and need to be fed often. Be on the lookout for roving meter maids in their little electric golf carts. Parking tickets start at $18 and then multiply after 30 unpaid days, even on rental cars. In South Beach, the best bet is to dump the car far from Ocean Drive. But don't park in the residential zones (which are marked with white signs) after 6pm daily, because the big, bad tow trucks will take your car away. In the Grove, it's better to park in on-street spaces, away from Cocowalk. But don't stray too far, because some of the surrounding areas are unsafe. Perhaps your best bet is to park the car in a parking garage. Rates range from $3 to $10 for an evening.

Public transportation... Getting around Miami can be a headache if you use the public transportation system: late buses, broken-down systems, dirty seats. Don't say we didn't warn you. **Metrorail** is a 21-mile-long elevated train that runs north to south through downtown every 20 minutes, until midnight. The fare is $1.25; transfers are 25¢. **Metromover** is much like Disneyland's monorail. It runs a 4.5-mile downtown loop, offers great city views, and costs 25¢. **Metrobuses** criss-cross and lumber all over Dade County, covering 2,000 miles and—in doing so—are often late. Then again, schedules can be a little off, so you should try to get to the stop at least 10 minutes early. Bus stops are marked by green-and-blue signs with a bug logo. Bus fares are $1.25 and transfers are 25¢. To really prepare yourself for this kind of transit torture, you can write for the *First-Time Rider's Kit* (tel 305/638–6700; Metropolitan Dade County Transit Authority, 3300 N.W. 32nd Ave., Miami 33142). Or you can pick one up at the Greater Miami Convention and Visitors Bureau (tel 305/539–3063 or 800/283—2707; 701 Brickell Ave., Miami 33131).

Radio... Catering to Miami's multi-ethnic tastes, there's something for everyone to listen to on both sides of the dial. Music stations on the FM dial are: **WLRN (91.3)**, the National Public Radio affiliate; **WTMI (93.1)** spins classic classical; **WLVE (93.9)** is jazz and soft stuff; **WKIS (99.9)** plays country; **WMJK (102.7)** plays the oldies; **WZTA (94.9)** is classic rock with a new edge; **WVUM (90.5)** is the University of Miami's student station, playing alternative rave music; **WHYY (100.7)** offers Top 40 cuts, and **WPOW (96.5)** has dance music. **WQBA (107.5)** and **WXOJ (95)** air Spanish tunes with Spanglish-speaking deejays. It's a good way to pick up some Spanish while you're in Mee-ahm-mee. The big talk stations are on the AM band: **WIOD (610)**, **WNWS (790)**, **WJNO (1230)**, and **WPBR (1340)**.

Smoking... Florida law prohibits smoking in public buildings, so you'll see folks lighting up outside office buildings and businesses. Most restaurants have gone "PC" and added nonsmoking sections, and many hotels have nonsmoking room, as well.

Taxes... Goods and services purchased in Dade County are taxed at 6.5 percent. Many of the tourist towns like Miami Beach, Bal Harbour, and Surfside impose their own supplemental taxes and call them resort, development, or professional-sports-facility taxes. Taxes range from 9.5 to 11.5 percent.

Taxis... Cabbies' meters click on at $1.10 and charge about $1.75 a mile. Flat fees, based on zones, are charged for transport to and from the airport. From Miami Beach to MIA (Miami International Airport), for example, the bill would be about $22. Taxis are also radio-dispatched, so if you see one coming your way, it will most likely whoosh right by you. To hail one, yell "Oye mang!" while flapping your arms, and hope the driver will pull over. (It works for some folks, but it's not guaranteed.) If it doesn't stop, hang out at one of the hotels and shopping centers where cabs congregate. Or call **American Taxi** (tel 305/947–3333), **Central Taxi** (tel 305/532–5555), **Diamond Cab** (tel 305/545–7575), **Metro Taxi** (tel 305/888–8888), or **Yellow Cab** (tel 305/444–4444).

Tickets... TicketMaster (tel 305/358–5885) lets you charge tickets by phone, to theater, music, and sporting events.

Time and temperature... For local time and weather, call 305/324–8811.

Tipping... Here's a Miami tip: The city was recently ranked by some poll as sixth among the top-35 U.S. tipping cities. Standard gratuity for waiters and bartenders is 15 percent. Unless you're a tightwad, most local waiters aspire to a 20-percent tip. Be aware that many Miami Beach restaurants have adopted the European custom of adding a 15-percent gratuity to your bill. If you don't tip the airport porters about $1 per bag they'll sneer and scowl at you, which is not the best way to start your stay here. If you do tip them, they'll hail a taxi for you.

Trains... Green double-decker **Tri-Rail trains** (tel 305/728–8445 or 800/874–7245) connect Dade, Broward, and Palm Beach counties. They're the closest thing to bullet trains South Florida has to offer, and you may see them rolling along I-95. For long-distance trains, **Amtrak** (tel 305/835–1222; 8303 N.W. 37th Ave.) has a station in a seedy part of town.

Traveler's aid... This service (tel 305/448–8228; 1790 SW 27th Ave., Miami 33145) provides emergency assistance to travelers who meet with emergencies during their stays. In dire need, you can turn to them for crisis intervention and counseling, help with finding shelter and food, and assistance with replacing travel documents.

TV stations... The networks: **ABC** is Channel 10, **CBS** is Channel 4, **NBC** is Channel 6, **Fox** is Channel 7, and **PBS** is Channel 2. The two largest Spanish-language TV stations are **Univision**, Channel 23, and **Telemundo**, Channel 51.

Visitor information... Although not open at night, you can plan ahead with **The Greater Miami Convention and Visitors Bureau** (tel 305/539–3063 or 800/283–2707; 701 Brickell Ave., Miami, 33133; and tel 305/577–3334; 401 Biscayne Blvd. at Bayside Marketplace, Miami

33132); **The Miami Design Preservation League Welcome Center** (tel 305/531–3484; 1001 Ocean Dr. Miami Beach 33139); **The Coconut Grove Chamber of Commerce** (tel 305/444–7270; 2820 MacFarlane Rd., Coconut Grove 33133); **The Coral Gables Chamber of Commerce** (tel 305/446–1657; 50 Aragon Ave., Coral Gables 33134), **Greater Miami Chamber of Commerce** (tel 305/539–3063; Omni International, 1601 Biscayne Blvd., Miami 33132); and **The Miami Beach Chamber of Commerce** (tel 305/672–1270; 1920 Meridian Ave., Miami Beach 33139).